In the beginning,

there were only the basics (pigs, olives, squids), hungry people bored of the same dishes and a cooking flame. From this modest mix, an array of hearty, wholesome and tasty dishes were produced. Not only did they feed the masses — and cheaply to boot — but they prepared the ground rules for the techniques and flavours found in today's cooking. Greg dons a peasant robe, dips into this history and rediscovers some of the most delicious meals created from the humblest beginnings.

The Pig, the Olive & the Squid

To my mum — who taught me
to be thrifty and to improvise

Published in 2007 by Murdoch Books Pty Limited
www.murdochbooks.com.au

Murdoch Books Australia
Pier 8/9, 23 Hickson Road
Millers Point, NSW 2000
Phone: +61 (0) 2 8220 2000
Fax: +61 (0) 2 8220 2558

Murdoch Books UK Limited
Erico House, 6th Floor
93–99 Upper Richmond Road
Putney, London SW15 2TG
Phone: +44 (0) 20 8785 5995
Fax: +44 (0) 20 8785 5985

Chief Executive: Juliet Rogers
Publishing Director: Kay Scarlett

Project Manager: Colette Vella
Design Concept, Art Direction and Design: Lauren Camilleri
Editor: Paul McNally
Production: Maiya Levitch
Photographer: John Fryz
Stylists: Jo Briscoe (cover, endpapers and pages 6, 11, 12, 43, 65, 68, 79, 82, 87, 96, 128, 138, 143, 152); and Simon Bajada (pages 36, 50, 55, 60, 74, 90, 102, 114, 122, 132, 137, 146, 157)
Food Preparation: Ross Dobson

A catalogue record for this book is available from the National Library of Australia and the British Library.

ISBN 978 1 9212 0859 1

Printed by 1010 Printing International Limited in 2007. Printed in China.

Conversion Guide: You may find cooking times vary depending on the oven you are using. We have used 20 ml (4 teaspoon) tablespoon measures. If you are using a 15 ml (3 teaspoon) tablespoon, for most recipes the difference will not be noticeable. However, for recipes using baking powder, gelatine, bicarbonate of soda (baking soda), small amounts of flour and cornflour (cornstarch), add an extra teaspoon for each tablespoon specified.

The Pig, the Olive & the Squid

FOOD & WINE FROM HUMBLE BEGINNINGS

greg duncan powell

MURDOCH BOOKS

Table of Contents

Preface

When I was younger, I was less concerned with cooking than I was with self-sufficiency. At the age of 16 I began my first experiment. Winter 1978. School holidays. I stayed in a caravan on the south coast of New South Wales for two weeks with a surfboard, a wetsuit, a packet of Uncle Toby's oats, a fishing rod, three Thomas Hardy novels, a book on self-sufficiency and a $10 note. The plan was to get everything I needed from the sea.

It all began well. The first time I dropped the line in I caught a blackfish. It was going to be a cinch. But then the fish stopped biting. I found myself eating porridge three times a day. I studied my self-sufficiency book and explored the shoreline, tasting various naturally occurring edible (and inedible) substances. Pigface — edible as it said in the book, but a purgative as it also advised. I experimented with various types of seaweed — too salty even after soaking in fresh water 20 times. The various tiny rock molluscs were edible once you removed the sand but were nibbles, not main course.

The problem was that I wasn't devoting all my time to food gathering. I was surfing five or six hours a day and consuming calories that I couldn't replace. Finally hunger and porridge-fatigue won. I broke into my emergency $10 and bought a packet of rice, a bag of onions and half a pound of butter. It was then that I started to really cook — flavouring various strange paellas and risottos with molluscs, seaweed and the herbs I stole from a nearby garden.

The self-sufficiency experiment failed but the whole exercise set me on a path from which I have never deviated. At university, poverty provided more opportunities for experimentation both from a historical (I was studying medieval history) and from an economic point of view. Pasta with a sauce made from oil and garlic (you'll find the recipe here), curries that were not vegetarian but were made with almost no meat (there's a few of them here too), and a multitude of hearty medieval minestrones. This food might sound humble or even peasant-like, but what I was saving on groceries I was spending on wine. Not just because I was besotted with wine by that stage, but also because it made such a difference to what I cooked. That was the big discovery. A simple bottle of cheap wine could make my pasta with oil and garlic taste like food from a fancypants Italian restaurant. Wine is the missing link — the ingredient that is never mentioned in the recipe.

Introduction

One of the quickest ways to understand a person — apart from looking in their sock drawer — is to look in their kitchen cupboards, or better still, observe them at work behind the stove. Scrutinize the way they slice, cut and chop, the knife they choose, the mess that ensues and how that mess is dealt with, and you will know the inner person.

This sort of kitchen audition is a far more accurate and effective way to evaluate the compatibility of a future partner than astrology or palm reading, but there's as much to learn in why someone cooks as in *how* someone cooks. Once a human being can throw a few bits and pieces in a saucepan and keep starvation at bay, cooking takes on entirely a new motivation. A person can cook to impress, to thrill, to woo, to relax, to please, to purge, to control, to divert, to drink, to think — there are hundreds of reasons why someone will take to the kitchen.

I cook for various reasons but one of them is to link myself to all the cooking that has gone before. I like the idea that I'm connecting through food to all places and all times. As a person living in 2007 I'm obviously very different to someone stirring a pot in 1519, but if we're both cooking cabbage soup we are in some way connected. We share the need to eat and the urge to create — the same two forces that shaped food culture then and shape food culture now.

Most cooks don't realize that when they cook they're playing with history. But like most things on earth, the food we eat has evolved. It has a linear chronology. Our food culture, no matter how clever or sophisticated or multicultural, is the result of all that has gone before and all that has driven it — fashions, famines and feasts.

Most of the recipes that have survived through to today were not the food of the rich and wealthy — the best recipes tend to be born out of necessity. When ingredients are limited the most important ingredient is ingenuity. It's like poetry. Cooking with a fully stocked pantry is like writing poetry that doesn't rhyme — it's too easy. Ingenuity isn't a necessity. But take a cup of rock-hard chickpeas, clean out the vegie drawer of the fridge and add some inspiration — to me that's a challenge and that's the true and forgotten essence of cooking.

That sort of cooking is magic. It's sow's ear into silk purse — or at least sow's ear into pork sausage — magic. In this sense a cook is an alchemist, a sorcerer. A cook is also an interior decorator who, with a saucepan simmering on the stove, can turn a house into a home. But a clever cook is also an economist, a financial planner, an accountant and an events organizer. With a little skill, a frugal chef can defy the CPI.

Cooking to a budget is a much neglected part of the art. It used to be that when we learned how to cook, we didn't learn how to be a chef, we learned 'home economics' — or at least the girls did. While the boys were making a mess in woodwork, the girls preserved fruit, cooked corned beef or made marmalade, and always under the mantra, 'waste not, want not'.

It wasn't chefery, as we know it today — whiz-bang wokking or flashy knife work — it was the basics. Home economics addressed what have been the cook's main challenges since the beginning of time: preservation, creation, conservation and what to do with the leftovers. When man discovered fire and barbecued his first dinosaur T-bone it would have been a great moment. But after the feasting finished he faced those very same problems cooks have faced for centuries:

1. *What to do with the leftover dinosaur so it didn't go off.*
2. *How to cook it in a different way so that the tribe didn't get bored with dinosaur for breakfast, lunch and dinner.*
3. *How to cook all the bits of dinosaur so that none was wasted.*
4. *Who would do the washing up.*

This book addresses all but the last point — you're going to have to sort that one out for yourself. Each chapter focuses on a single classic ingredient and different ways to cook and serve it, always with an eye on the budget — and the glass of wine you're going to drink with it. If you never had an Italian, Greek, Portuguese, Spanish, Indian, French (or any other non-Anglo nationality) grandmother to take you in hand and show you the ancient secrets of her kitchen, and you like to drink wine with food, this is the book for you.

Chapter I
The Grape

It was once said of salt that it makes its presence felt by its absence. Apparently, if deprived of salt for too long, humans have a tendency to chew dirt. I feel very much the same way about wine. Bereft of wine I might not actually eat soil, but metaphorically my dinners would be dirt. Without wine, food is soulless. There's nothing to lift it off the plate apart from the basic mechanics of fork and spoon. Eating food without wine is refuelling, it's not feasting. Every meal is breakfast. Life is a permanent Methodist picnic, an eternal weekend with your teetotaller auntie.

A wine-less existence is almost too horrible to contemplate. Humans and wine are, after all, inseparable. The relationship goes back thousands of years. The first evidence of cultivated vines are found in the republic of Georgia and date back to 7000–5000 BC. But winemaking was going on way before then. Fossilized grape pips have been found in piles, suggesting winemaking dates back to the Stone Age. It's not surprising. Wine didn't need to be the result of some Neanderthal brainwave — it would have invented itself. After all, the difference between a bucket of grapes and a bucket of fermenting wine is but a few hot days or a clumsy foot.

It's not difficult to make wine from grapes but have you ever asked yourself, 'why grapes?' Why not peaches, lychees or pomegranates? It's true that 'wine' can be made from pretty much anything — even broccoli if so desired — but not without the addition of sugar. A ripe grape is the only fruit with enough natural sugar to produce enough alcohol to make a liquid that will be relatively stable and keep bacteria at bay. No wonder that in pre-refrigeration times, when most of what went into people's bellies was off or nearly off, wine was regarded as medicine.

Wine is made from grapes but the real credit should go to *Vitis vinifera*, a truly amazing plant. There are some 40 odd sub-genus of *Vitis* — the grape vine. There's *Vitis riparia* (from river banks) and *Vitis rupestris* (rock loving) to name a few, but the one that has spread throughout the world and given so much pleasure is *Vitis vinifera*, which means 'wine bearing'.

Vitis vinifera evolved from vines from the Asian *Vitis* species, and the thing that now distinguishes *vinifera* from its wild Asian cousins is that its genes are heterozygous. An excellent Scrabble word, heterozygous means that an organism will not breed true to type — its genes are constantly in a state of flux. This makes the grape vine surprisingly adaptable. But not only is it heterozygous, it's also a hermaphrodite. Wild vines are a mixture of fruitless males and fruiting females but not *vinifera*; she (or he) has done away with the need for bees and can propagate vegetatively, and bud mutation is very common.

Forgive the botanical tangent but this stuff is important — it's where the whole thing gets interesting. The mutating grapevine is the reason for all the different varieties, for all the different tastes, for all the talk of 'terroir', for my livelihood and for wine tosserdom in general. It is the unstable nature of the vine that makes viticulture and winemaking so interesting and makes wine so much more than fermented fruit juice. Without those mutations and the subtle (and not so subtle) differences, we might be drinking it, but we wouldn't be talking about it, showing off about it or writing about it.

an early history of wine connoisseurship

"*First there was a boar from Lucania which our gracious host kept telling us was caught in a soft southerly breeze. It was garnished with things that stimulate jaded appetite — lettuces, spicy turnips, radishes, skirret, fish pickle and the lees of Coan wine. Then like an attic maiden bearing the holy emblems of Ceres, in came the dark Hydaspes carrying Caecuban wine, followed by Alcon with unsalted Chian. Then his lordship said, 'If you prefer Falernian or Alban to what had been served ... we do have both varieties.'*"

HORACE, BOOK II SATIRE 8

The wine tosser is not a new species. They are as old as wine itself. Way back in 1 BC when Horace — a self-confessed wine tosser — satirized them, wine snobbery was fully developed. Roman senators dropped names, described flavours in flowery language and talked 'terroir' as if they themselves worked the land. They were clued up on the famous vintages, such as the supposedly wonderful Opimium vintage of 121 BC (so named because Opimius was the consul for that year). Even the lifestyle of the 'gentleman vigneron' seems to have appealed to the same sorts of people as it does today. Owning one's own vineyard became a rich man's hobby, much as it is now with doctors and lawyers. The emperor Julian even planted a vineyard with his own hands and then bequeathed it to a friend as 'a modest souvenir of my gardening'.

In fact, the only difference between the wine scene then and now, apart from small details such as the use of amphorae and the lack of Riedel stemware, were the wines. Some of the descriptions sound a bit strange to our tastes: 'brown liquids which take light when flame is applied to them' and wines 'bitter and impossible to drink without adding water'. But these sorts of descriptions were unusual. The Roman palate had a sweet tooth and the food they prized was flavoured almost out of recognition with such diverse ingredients as honey and fermented fish sauce, so it's not surprising that the wines they favoured tended to be unctuous and sweet.

Many of the great vineyards of Rome still exist but no longer seem to produce the wines that Pliny and his mates raved about. The famous Falernian is still made where it was, and is still amber in colour but not very good. Alban exists now as Frascati — that lean, rather bland Italian white grown southeast of Rome. But Caecuban is no longer — the vineyards were dug up during Nero's reign because he believed there was treasure lying underneath.

The legacy of Roman wine styles may not have been passed on but the culture of the vine has. Where the Roman Empire spread so did *Vitis vinifera*. Resettling veteran soldiers planted vineyards in far-flung corners of the Empire and passed the whole addictive culture of wine and vine growing on to the local tribes. The Gauls, Vandals and Visigoths may not have been interested in many of the trappings of Roman civilization but in most cases when they sacked, burned and raped, they left the vineyards, wineries and those who worked them alone. The Roman viticulture manuals recommended vines be tied to stakes the height of a man, with rows of vines two paces wide and two paces apart, and that's still the way many vineyards are laid out all over Europe. Thankfully, there was one light burning in the Dark Ages. While the Roman civilization was collapsing, the present European vine-scape began to take shape.

Later, as the Christian Church established itself during the Merovingian and Carolingian eras, the vine found other custodians. Monasteries and wine have a long connection, both in cultivation and consumption. Saint Benedict, who founded the Benedictine order in AD 529, recommended about half a pint of wine per day for each monk, but was prepared to be a bit flexible depending on the monk's constitution. The monasteries produced it and the powerful bishops fought over those dioceses that produced the best wine.

During the late 12th and early 13th centuries Europe changed. It was a renaissance (before the bigger one later) and was the time when the whole idea of chivalry and romantic love took hold. It was about then that a hierarchy of wine regions began to evolve. A poem written in 1224 called 'La Bataille des vins', by one Henry d'Andeli, tells the story of a competition conducted by the then King of France. At the time there was increasing rivalry between the wines of northern France, which were lighter and white, and those of the south, which were stronger and red. These days you'd drink the former with oysters and the latter with steak, but such ideas were still very foreign. Seventy samples from as far away as Spain and Germany competed with wines from Alsace, Bordeaux, Champagne, Burgundy and many other places in France that don't have a reputation for wine. One person — an English priest personally selected by the King — decided the fate of each of the competitors. In the black-and-white world of medieval Europe there were only winners or losers, good or evil, and at the behest of the priest, the wines were either pronounced 'celebrated' or 'excommunicated'.

While wines were being excommunicated on the basis of their quality, the whole notion of description to prove or disprove the quality or worth of a wine was beginning to take hold. They tended to lay more emphasis on the healthful or poisonous effects of the beverage than on colour, nose and palate. In the late 12th century, physician Arnaldus de Villanova wrote *Liber de Vinis* — a guide to wine tasting from a medical and practical point of view. It pointed out all the tricks and devices winesellers employed (and still employ) to sell wine — a version of the 'buy with apples, sell with cheese' formula. The book offers practical information for improving bad wines, but also ascribes to certain wines magical or medical properties — the curing of the insane, rectifying the sinews and making hair grow.

Some of the prose we recognize as 'wine writing' emerged during the 13th century. A tasting note survives from the Irish linguist and Dominican, Geoffrey of Waterford. His rather poetic tasting note for Vernache or Vernaccia (a white wine still surviving in central Italy) reads: 'it opens out sweetly as it comes into the mouth, greets the nostrils and comforts the brain, taking the palate softly but with force'.

Another friar utilizing pen and palate to great effect was the Catalan Franciscan, Fancesc Eiximenis, who wrote on many subjects but gave particular vent to his patriotism and disgust for wine tossers. 'Only the Catalan nation is an example to others in the way of tempered correct drinking' he writes, and compares his countrymen to the Italians who

"*drink in stages and small quantities at a time, examining and re-examining the wine just as physicians do with urine, and they taste it repeatedly, chewing it slowly between their teeth until they have drunk it all.*"

With the advent of pathology labs, most physicians no longer have to taste the urine of their patients, but apart from that, the Catalan friar has given a picture perfect description of a 21st century wine industry professional. This is exactly how myself and most of my colleagues taste wine — even when we're not actually working. As I said at the start, the wine tosser is not a new species.

wine: the forgotten condiment

Look in your kitchen cupboards and you'll find plenty of things that make food taste better: salt, pepper, spices, sauces … but what about wine? Few people put it in the cupboard, or in the same category. Yet it is the ultimate condiment. It can make relatively ordinary food taste extraordinary and can make forgettable food memorable. A basic cheese omelette eaten with a cup of tea is completely different from one eaten with a glass of Champagne. With the French fizz, an omelette morphs from a dish of fluffy fried eggs to fancy restaurant fare. But, you say, doesn't everything taste better with a glass of expensive French fizz? On the contrary, Champagne won't do a meat pie any favours and vice versa. It's about combinations. Swap the bubbly for a glass of cheap pinot and you'll wonder why every meat pie isn't consumed with it. The right wine can take ordinary food into another realm. A souvlaki from your local Greek takeaway almost tastes exotic with a glass of reasonable cask red — instead of the colicky cola traditionally provided. The truth is that be it a simple barbecued sausage or a freshly peeled prawn or shrimp, consumption with wine is the finishing touch — which is, too often, also the missing touch. Wine is the forgotten condiment and is available in hundreds of different flavours — or grape varieties, if you prefer. Following are a few of the commonly available ones.

meet your table partners

ARNEIS An almost extinct Piedmontese white wine grape that, in a bizarre turn of fate, will probably become more popular in Australia than it ever was in Italy. Arneis is a fairly understated fellow. He has a full body with good length and hints at fragrances of pears, almond and occasionally honeysuckle.

BARBERA Barbie, as she's familiarly known, is the queen of the food wines. She is a red Italian variety from Piedmont. Relatively light in comparison to a shiraz, she can be quite edgy and acidic before the food arrives, but with food she's charming.

CABERNET FRANC This is cabernet sauvignon's congenial cousin. He mostly sits in the background in blends and lets bossy cab sauv do most of the talking. He has similar sorts of flavours along blackcurrant lines, but is a little less boisterous in the tannin department.

CABERNET SAUVIGNON A distinguished red grape, which if it wore clothes would probably go with the blue blazer. Unlike shiraz, which can have a rustic, earthy side, Mr C. Sauvignon likes it best in the posh wine regions — Coonawarra in South Australia, Margaret River in Western Australia and those sorts of places, where his cedary blackcurrant flavours come to the fore.

CHAMBOURCIN This is a hybrid red grape championed because of its resistance to fungal diseases. It's like seedless watermelons and modern tomatoes — a bit tasteless. It's best for light, cheap reds — or chopping down with a chainsaw.

CHARDONNAY Chardonnay is the most famous and most planted white grape in the world. It's supremely adaptable to a wide range of climates yet retains its distinctive chardie characteristics. Whether matured in French oak as a still wine or used to make sparkling wine, chardonnay deserves its aristocratic status and remains one of the greatest mutations of the *Vitis vinifera*.

CHENIN BLANC This is pretty sauvignon blanc's plainer sister. With not as much flavour or personality, her saving grace is that she can be much more subtle than her boastful, bragging sister. Good Australian versions are rare, and unless you like experimenting, leave chenin on the shelf.

COLOMBARD This is one of those neutral, pleasant tasting white varieties that suits an arid, warm climate and has prospered without much fanfare. Clever winemakers use it as a blending option.

DOLCETTO A red variety from Piedmont whose name translates as 'little sweet one', dolcetto's black–purple colour might suggest a huge red, so her soft, succulent, easy drinkability comes as a surprise. Her forte is as a luncheon red.

DURIF This is an underrated hybrid red grape created by Dr Durif. A powerful red with the savour of shiraz and the tannic grunt of cabernet, it works particularly well in warmer climates. In the United States it's known as petite syrah — a name that seems ironic.

GEWÜRZTRAMINER Gewürztraminer is a somewhat effeminate white German who wears loads of aftershave. Aromas of talc and rose petal waft from him. Occasionally fantastic but fairly difficult with food, he's for devotees only.

GRENACHE A red grape originally from Spain and known there as garnacha, grenache moved to France and became famous in the Cotes du Rhone, especially when blended with shiraz. Grenache has a sweet fruity flavour that tends to come into its own as a foil to shiraz' savoury qualities.

MARSANNE A white grape from the Rhone Valley in France, which has achieved some fame in parts of Victoria. When picked not too ripe, the wine has some cellaring potential — as long as you pick the unwooded variety.

MERLOT Her name is pretty and easy to pronounce, she sounds nice, and the whole idea of a plump, fleshy red without too much tannin is very appealing — but in most cases she's a disappointment. Merlot is one of those varieties that prove the truism that if the demand is strong the wine is weak.

MUSCAT This is a grape that crosses the threshold between table grape and wine grape. There is a whole family of muscat and a range of wines produced from it; the most famous wine style is moscato, a grapey, slightly sweet, semi fizzy wine, which is low in alcohol.

NEBBIOLO An intriguing northern Italian who produces some of that country's greatest red wines, notably Barolo and Barbaresco. The rather washed out, pale colour belies a stubborn, strong personality and loads of backbone. Cellaring potential is high and all that tannin makes him a great red for strongly-flavoured Italian food.

PETIT VERDOT Little verdot is a red grape from Bordeaux in France that likes the heat. Consequently he's very happy in the warmer parts of Australia and produces firm, tasty red wines.

PINOT GRIGIO/GRIS Pinot grigio is the Italian version of this white grape and is usually made to a lighter, more lithe, less alcoholic style; pinot gris is the French version from Alsace and, true to that region's cuisine, is fuller bodied.

PINOT NOIR Dubbed the holy grail by frustrated winemakers, pinot noir is a red grape from Burgundy renowned for being finicky and fussy. Picky pinot only performs in cool climates and prefers to yield very little. When everything is right, it is the most sublime and ethereal of red wines.

RIESLING A German white variety of undoubted class. For a long time riesling has been living down a bad reputation in Australia due to some very crappy wines (some that weren't even made from riesling). Crisp, floral and citrus, riesling is arguably Australia's greatest white wine.

SANGIOVESE With a name that translates as 'blood of Jupiter', it's no surprise this is Italy's favourite red grape. It's the grape responsible for chianti, and is notorious for mutating into not-so-good versions of itself. It makes medium-bodied red wines of exquisite texture and food compatibility.

SAUVIGNON BLANC Sauvignon blanc gets its name from 'savage' or 'wild'. This may refer to its native origins, the boisterous growing habit or even the rambunctious flavours and zippy zestiness, which are quite wild. Sauvignon blanc is the white variety of the moment.

SEMILLON Semillon is an intriguing white grape. While she can seem nondescript, lean and rather plain, she has the bone structure to age fantastically.

SHIRAZ Shiraz, or syrah as the French prefer, is arguably the most versatile, utilitarian red grape. Adaptable to warm and reasonably cool climates, he's reliable and a good all rounder.

TEMPRANILLO Tempranillo is to Spain what shiraz is to Australia and what sangiovese is to Italy. Tempranillo's most famous expression is rioja. With a bit of the texture of sangiovese and, when mature, something of the aroma of pinot noir, the stylish Spaniard is a latecomer to Australia's wine scene but is settling in nicely.

VIOGNIER Viognier is a trendy white grape from the Rhone Valley, which can be used in two ways. It can make a honeyed, luscious white wine, but is also added to shiraz in very small amounts to make seductively perfumed, very drinkable, shiraz.

three easy rules to choosing the best wines

Most people can tell the difference between good wine and bad wine. Given the choice between an average product and something a bit better, the majority can pick the quality beverage. Listening to your senses is not really that difficult — the trickiest part is remembering what you drank. I'm not referring to overindulgence — that's a separate issue altogether — it's about those little details: name, vintage, region and grape variety(ies). I've had hundreds of 'conversations' that go something like this:

"
Them: I had a really fantastic wine the other night.
Me: What was it?
Them: It had a blue label.
Me: What was the name on the label?
Them: There was running writing and a picture of a castle …"

If you're recognizing yourself here, don't despair. Most normal people (i.e. non-professionals) drink wine as they chat about more important stuff. At first sip, the wine is noted as good or bad and then forgotten. Most people's brains are already too overstocked to absorb extraneous wine details. Visual memory comes to the rescue and this is the way most people buy wine. It's estimated that more than 80 per cent of wine is purchased because the label appeals or is recognized. Consequently, wineries have come up with many ingenious and not so ingenious ways to try to lodge their brand in the consumer consciousness: garish, luminous labels and catchy names such as Dead Man's Ditch instead of the more traditional Mountain View Brook Estates. One large company has even gone to the extent of incorporating little stickers onto their labels that you're meant to peel off and put in your handbag/pocket for future reference. Anecdotal evidence proves that these don't work either. The sorts of people who remember to peel off the sticker after drinking a bottle of wine and then remember to get it out of their pocket before the pants go in the wash are normally the sort of organized types who would have pulled out pen and paper and written the name of the wine down anyway.

RULE 1 — BEWARE OF PONCY PACKAGING

To buy good wine and drink well, you don't have to commit vast slabs of information to memory and you don't have to plough through turgid wine columns. You do need to ignore the label. Either shut off the visual side of the brain or use the label's appeal in a more critical way. If it attracts your eye and looks like a multitude of talented graphic artists and clever marketing people have been employed in its creation, it means that the money didn't go into the grapes.

RULE 2 — DON'T TRY TO REMEMBER THE NAME OF THE WINE

Don't worry about remembering vintages either. In Australia there isn't a huge variation year to year and with global warming most vintages are dry and hot. The same goes for brand names. Don't bother too much about these. There are almost 2000 wineries in Australia, many of which have several labels under the one roof. They change hands, change names and come and go, and to remember every winery name uses a lot of mental gigabytes.

RULE 3 — DO TRY TO REMEMBER SUCCESSFUL COMBINATIONS OF REGIONS AND GRAPE VARIETIES

The most helpful thing in buying wine is to recognize and memorize successful combinations of wine region and grape variety. Know this and you can't go wrong. Given that the winemaking is professional (as it almost always is), a correct matching of region to grape variety is usually the reason a wine tastes good. It's all about the intricate workings of different grape varieties and particular climates, soils and seasons. The Australian wine industry is relatively young — only 180 years or thereabouts — and is still experimental. This means that we're still working out what grape varieties are best suited to which bits of the country. Europe had a thousand years head start on us and has already got that all sorted. However, in the last 20 years it has all become a lot clearer, and there has emerged a definitive class of combinations which, year by year, not only offer the best quality but a consistent style and range of flavours. Knowing what to expect before you pull the cork or screw the cap doesn't mean that there are no surprises — each wine from each year is still unique — but it's invaluable in trying to match wines with food.

13 of the best Australian grape and region combos

1. TASMANIAN SPARKLING WINE

Australia's smallest state is fast becoming Australia's Champagne. Launceston is Rheims and Hobart is Epernay … well not quite, but the cool summers and long ripening periods of Tasmania are proving perfect for the growing of chardonnay and pinot noir (the official grapes of Champagne) for sparkling wine. The key requirement for good bubbly is natural acidity — and that only comes from cool climates. It is that acidity that gives a sparkling wine poise, balance and airy finesse, which is absolutely crucial to the style.

2. CLARE VALLEY RIESLING

The Clare Valley lies to the northeast of Adelaide, just before South Australia becomes desert, and is one of Australia's quaintest wine regions and home to Australia's most reliable riesling. Clare rieslings are limey, minerally wines. They reward cellaring for several years and when drunk young make fantastic seafood wines.

3. ADELAIDE HILLS SAUVIGNON BLANC OR MARLBOROUGH, NEW ZEALAND, SAUVIGNON BLANC

Sauv blanc isn't my favourite grape variety but I'm in the minority — it's hugely popular. If you're a sauv blanc fan these are the two regions to buy them from. Long, slow ripening is the key to flavour and structure.

4. HUNTER VALLEY SEMILLON

A unique wine style, Hunter semillon evolved by accident. The Hunter, located just north of Sydney, isn't the ideal grape-growing region and it often rains just before harvest time. Imminent rain often led cloud-watching vignerons to harvest their fruit before complete ripeness. Voila! The Hunter semillon wine style was born. Clean, lean, citric, low in alcohol but fantastic with cold seafood, and with the acidity to guarantee longevity in the cellar — it is, as I said, unique.

5. YARRA VALLEY CHARDONNAY

There are quite a few regions that can legitimately claim to produce great chardonnay. The Adelaide Hills in South Australia and Margaret River in Western Australia do a pretty good job, but dollar for dollar the most consistent ones come out of the

Yarra in Victoria. If everyone drank Yarra chardonnay the variety would be much less maligned. Some cleverly run professional wineries with quite a bit of experience means that the duds are few and far between.

6. COOL CLIMATE PINOT GRIGIO

It's early days for pinot grigio and it is yet to find its perfect spot in Australia, but good ones are emerging from most cool climates — Tasmania, and the Victorian areas of the Mornington Peninsula and the King Valley. It's a useful white wine, particularly with food, and is destined to reach great heights as our winemakers and regions come to grips with it.

7. RIVERINA BOTRYTIS SEMILLON

The inland towns of Griffith and Leeton in New South Wales are the capitals of 'noble rot'. The long, dry autumns are perfect for botrytis to shrivel the semillon and add all those marmalade and dried apricot flavours so beloved of stickyophiles. At both the cheap and expensive end of the scale, it's difficult to find better stickies or better value outside the Riverina.

8. YARRA VALLEY PINOT NOIR

There are plenty of cool places in Australia that can produce a worthy pinot noir but not with the consistency of flavour and cost-effectiveness of the Yarra Valley in Victoria. Prices have fallen in recent years so it's not difficult to get a decent pinot for a small price. Affordable pinot is a good all-purpose food wine. It's equally at home with a lamb chop or a bit of barbecued salmon.

9. KING VALLEY SANGIOVESE

The pretty King Valley in northeast Victoria is fast becoming Australia's Italy — at least where grapes are concerned. Once upon a time, winemakers treated sangiovese like shiraz and the results weren't very nice, but things have got better from both a winemaking and viticulture point of view. The Aussie chianti coming out of the King Valley makes a great post-modern barbecue red.

10. CENTRAL VICTORIAN SHIRAZ

There are many sub-regions in central Victoria, but where shiraz is concerned, the brief is the same: spicy, peppery, juicy and drinkable. Such a red is the ultimate house red — drinkable when relatively young, without the gargantuan proportions of Barossa shiraz, and particularly good with steak.

11. MCLAREN VALE SHIRAZ GRENACHE

Travelling in McLaren Vale, South Australia, you'll see old gnarled, untrellised vines — so-called bush vines. These are grenache vines, the secret behind this blend. This is a style of wine based on the red wine of the Cotes du Rhone. The Aussie version is a bit gutsier but suits full-on red meat dishes.

12. BAROSSA VALLEY CABERNET/SHIRAZ

The cabernet/shiraz blend is an Australian invention and something to be proud of. Most situations are improved by a bit of shiraz, and South Australian cabernet is no different. It fleshes out all the spots where cabernet is lacking and adds a few high notes and bass notes on the aroma front. The Barossa is where it all started and Barossans do it best.

13. MARGARET RIVER CABERNETS

If you're name dropping cabernet, Coonawarra is the traditional region associated with it, but in elegance, sheer class and cabernet upper-crustiness Western Australia's Margaret River is superior. They might be a bit lighter and you do have to pay some serious money for a good one, but the taste of a quality Margaret River cabernet stays in your olfactory memory forever.

● ● ● ● ● ● ● ● ● ● ● ●

Chapter 2
The Olive

When I first read Homer's *Odyssey*, one passage really appealed. Long suffering Odysseus had left another woman who wanted him to stay. He had raised the ire of Poseidon yet again and had been shipwrecked and dashed against an unknown shore — yet again. All briny and encrusted with salt he approaches some girls, including the young maiden Nausikaa (of the white arms) and convinces her to give him clothes and a flask of olive oil:

" *Stand as you are girls, a little away from me so that I can wash the salt off my shoulders and use the olive oil on them. It is a long time since my skin has known any ointment. But I will not bathe in front of you, for I feel embarrassed in the presence of lovely-haired girls to appear all naked. But when great Odysseus had bathed in the river and washed from his body the salt brine, which clung to his back and broad shoulders, he scraped from his head the scurf of brine from the barren salt sea. But when he had bathed all, and anointed himself with olive oil, and put on the clothing this unwedded girl had given him, then Athene, daughter of Zeus, made him seem taller for the eye to behold and thicker, and on his head she arranged the curling locks that hung down like hyacinthine petals.* "

It's a typically Homeric piece of prose demonstrating the many ancient uses for olive oil — soap, ointment, shampoo, moisturizer, body lotion, hair-gel … It was this passage (and some ancient hero worship) that led me to emulate Odysseus and his methods of personal hygiene. In April 1984 I gave up soap for extra virgin olive oil.

At first it was addictive. The feeling was soothing — especially on the feet. Fully lubed, I gleamed like a freshly basted chook and felt like a warrior fresh from Troy. No more dry, cracked skin, no need for exfoliation, but a few other problems soon emerged. My greased, slicked hair didn't really hang like hyacinthine petals, and left a rather greasy residue on the pillow. Then there was the aroma of freshly tossed salad that followed me around — along with the dogs that would lick the oil off my legs. But the thing that finally put an end to the anointing was that no amount of wax could stop me slipping off my surfboard.

Barring a few silly examples, bathroom uses for olive oil never really made it out of the ancient world. Despite that, olive oil has entered a new golden age. The reason is simple. Research conducted into Mediterranean diets in the 1990s led to the rather obvious discovery that eating good food was good for you. That message has now been absorbed into the world's consciousness and non olive oil producing countries have been oiling their insides at a tremendous rate. Since 1990, when the research was first done, annual world olive production has increased from about one and a half million tonnes to almost three million.

Olive oil is the 21st century snake oil: the cure-all, the elixir of youth. Your heart condition will disappear, you'll live till you're 150, you'll be eloquent in most European languages, you'll have a better sex life, and be a favourite of the Gods. It worked for Odysseus.

It probably won't do any of that, but it might make you a better cook. Olive oil's organoleptic qualities make cooking easier. There are plenty of examples in this book where olive oil is the magic. Without it there is no recipe, just a bunch of ingredients. You can't say that about other fats. Then there's olive oil's physical make-up. Unlike most seed oils that change when heated and turn into toxic substances, olive oil remains true to its original form. There's also the phenomenon of crusting. When you fry with olive oil a crust forms on what you're frying, which makes the food tasty, but also stops what's being fried from becoming saturated with fat.

Unfortunately the cachet surrounding the whole subject of olives and their oil has now almost reached the same ridiculous levels as wine. It's got snob value, status and there are experts who intimidate others with their knowledge on the subject. There are olive oil tastings, lessons on how to taste olive oil, lessons on teaching others how to taste olive oil, and there's even an olive oil 'flavour wheel' to tell you the correct descriptors for what you taste.

Most of this detail becomes completely irrelevant once you fry your chips or mix in the balsamic. But some olive oil knowledge is useful. There are a host of words that get flung around on olive oil labels that seek to befuddle the consumer — 'light' for instance. Light oil does not contain fewer calories and is just rectified oil. 'Cold pressed' is another example. Almost no commercial oil is made by a traditional press anymore — it's all made by centrifuging. Beware — this is the commodity that introduced the notion of degrees of virginity. So, to clear up some misconceptions, here's the low-down on the different categories of oil according to the International Olive Oil Council.

OLIVE OIL is the oil obtained from the fruit of the olive tree solely by mechanical or other physical means under conditions, particularly thermal conditions, that do not lead to alterations in the oil, and which have not undergone any treatment other than washing, decantation, centrifugation and filtration.

EXTRA VIRGIN OLIVE OIL has less fatty acid than standard olive oil. It has a free acidity of not more than 0.8 grams per 100 grams. This means the smoking point is higher but that doesn't matter because extra virgin is rarely used for frying.

VIRGIN OLIVE OIL is slightly more acidic than extra virgin olive oil. It has a free acidity of not more than 2 grams per 100 grams.

REFINED OLIVE OIL is the olive oil obtained from virgin olive oils by refining methods that do not lead to alterations in the initial structure. It has a free acidity of not more than 0.3 grams per 100 grams and has one of the highest smoking points.

STANDARD OLIVE OIL is the oil consisting of a blend of refined olive oil and virgin olive oils. It has a free acidity of not more than 1 gram per 100 grams.

buying oil

The olive oil with the greatest reputation is Tuscan. It is delicate, fruity, peppery and lovely, but you have to pay a lot of money for the good stuff. Dollar for dollar I favour Portuguese oil — it's riper and heavier than the Italian stuff but packed with flavour. If you're buying in bulk, don't buy Italian. They're tasteless and rectified. Greek, Spanish — or if you can get it — Portuguese is best. If it's expensive extra virgin oil you're after, Italian is the best, but some local oils are really good too; and if you're purchasing for the bathroom, follow Odysseus' example and buy Greek.

Sauce de Sorges

THIS IS A VENERABLE SAUCE FROM ALSACE THAT IS PERFECT FOR ADDING FLAVOUR TO BOILED MEAT. IT'S FANTASTIC WITH POT AU FEU (PAGE 116) OR JUST ABOUT ANYTHING: SANDWICHES, SALADS, HOT DOGS — BUT NOT MEAT PIES.

MAKES 185 ML (6 FL OZ/¾ CUP)

Ingredients

ONE egg
TWO TEASPOONS lemon juice
TWO TEASPOONS dijon mustard
125 ML (4 FL OZ/½ CUP) olive oil
ONE TABLESPOON capers
ONE TABLESPOON chopped dill
TWO TABLESPOONS chopped flat-leaf (Italian) parsley

Method

First boil the egg for 3 minutes. Remove the yolk and beat it in a bowl. Save the white. Beat the lemon juice, mustard and a pinch of salt into the egg yolk. Slowly add the oil, drop by drop, until you're sure the mixture is blending and getting thicker, then you can add the oil a bit faster. Finally chop up the egg white and stir into the egg yolk with the capers, chopped dill and parsley. Keep in the fridge and bring up to room temperature or a bit below before serving.

Proper mayo

THE SUBJECT OF MAYONNAISE IS HIGHLY CONTROVERSIAL. LIKE MOST THINGS THAT ARE ANY GOOD IN THE WORLD OF COOKING, THE FRENCH THINK IT'S THEIRS, THE SPANISH ON THE OTHER HAND ARGUE THAT IT COMES FROM THE ISLAND OF MENORCA. THIS RECIPE IS THE SPANISH VERSION AND MAKING IT NEVER CEASES TO AMAZE. HOW CAN EGG YOLK, OIL, GARLIC AND A SHED LOAD OF HUMAN PATIENCE MAKE SUCH AN AMAZING SAUCE? A SAUCE THAT CAN TURN A LETTUCE LEAF, A DRIED UP PIECE OF FISH, OR AN OLD PRAWN OR SHRIMP INTO SOMETHING SUBLIME. IT'S ONE OF THOSE CONCOCTIONS THAT REQUIRES A LITTLE BIT OF VOODOO TO GET IT RIGHT. THE BEST RESULTS SEEM TO OCCUR DURING WANING MOONS, RISING TIDES AND WITH COOKS WHO HAVE RECENTLY CONFESSED THEIR SINS. I FIND STIRRING CLOCKWISE WITH THE LEFT HAND AND POURING IN THE OIL WITH THE RIGHT WORKS BEST — IF ONLY AS A SORT OF PENANCE. THE MOST IMPORTANT TIP IS TO MAKE SURE EGGS AND OIL ARE THE SAME TEMPERATURE. IF THE EGG HAS BEEN REFRIGERATED IT PROBABLY WON'T WORK. **MAKES 250 ML (9 FL OZ/1 CUP)**

Ingredients

TWO CLOVES garlic
ONE egg yolk
250 ML (9 FL OZ/1 CUP) good olive oil
lemon juice, to taste

Method

Crush the garlic in a mortar until soft and creamy. Remove to a bowl, add the egg yolk and mix them together. Now for the tricky bit: trickle the oil in very slowly, stirring in the same direction so that the oil and egg mix seamlessly together. If after a quarter of the oil has been poured in, the oil isn't thickening and you can see little bits of egg yolk in the liquid, it hasn't worked and isn't going to work. Save your oil and your arm and start all over again. If it is thickening, keep going until all the oil is blended and the mixture is thick and yellow. Add a little salt if you think it needs it and lemon juice to taste. Serve with anything you think needs a kick.

Spaghettini
aglio olio

I FIRST HAD THIS DISH IN AN ITALIAN RESTAURANT IN THE 1980'S WHEN I COULDN'T AFFORD ANYTHING ELSE ON THE MENU. I WAS SO IMPRESSED I ORDERED THE REAL DEAL IN VARIOUS FORMS WHEN I FINALLY MADE IT TO ITALY. LIKE ALL GREAT COMBINATIONS, THE FLAVOUR AND SATISFACTION FACTOR BELIES THE NUMBER OF INGREDIENTS. THE SMALLER THE DIAMETER OF PASTA THE BETTER IT TASTES, SO SPAGHETTINI IS BEST. DON'T USE FETTUCCINE. THIS IS A SPAG THAT GOES VERY WELL WITH CHEAP ITALIAN WINE, ESPECIALLY THOSE MADE FROM THE MONTEPULCIANO D'ABRUZZO GRAPE. **SERVES 4**

Ingredients

500 G (1 LB 2 OZ) spaghettini
FOUR TABLESPOONS tasty virginal olive oil
FOUR CLOVES garlic
LOTS of chopped flat-leaf (Italian) parsley

Method

Get a big saucepan of well-salted water boiling and add the spaghettini. Meanwhile, pour the olive oil into a heavy-based saucepan, add the garlic and heat over medium until the garlic starts to turn golden. Take off the heat and remove the garlic. When the pasta is *al dente*, drain. Heat the garlicky oil and mix it through the pasta. Finally, add the chopped parsley and some generous grinds of black pepper. Serve into heated bowls.

Açorda
alentejana

THIS IS ONE OF PORTUGAL'S FAMOUS SOUPS AND TYPIFIES PORTUGUESE COOKING: IT'S NOT VERY ATTRACTIVE, IS VERY SIMPLE TO MAKE, AND ENRICHES THE SOUL RATHER THAN THE SHAREHOLDERS OF MAJOR SUPERMARKETS. IT GOES REALLY WELL WITH RUSTIC, BASIC ITALIAN REDS OR LIGHTWEIGHT SHIRAZ/CABERNET BLENDS THAT HAVE BEEN OPENED FOR A WHILE. **SERVES 4**

Ingredients

ONE BUNCH coriander (cilantro), leaves and stems
THREE CLOVES garlic
FOUR TABLESPOONS virginal olive oil — Portuguese if you can get it
1.5 LITRES (52 FL OZ/6 CUPS) boiling water
HALF A LOAF stale, hard Italian-style bread
FOUR hard-boiled eggs

Method

In a mortar, mash the coriander, garlic and 1 tablespoon coarse salt into a green paste. Spoon the paste into a large saucepan, pour over the olive oil and add the boiling water. This is the base for the soup and is called the *açorda* or *sopa azeiteira* (olive oil soup). Adjust for seasoning, then add the bread cut into rough cubes and cover with a lid. Leave for a couple of minutes, then serve into four large bowls. Peel the eggs and slice one into each bowl. If you want to be really authentic, stir the soup with a bit of crusty old bread and taste the bread to adjust the seasoning.

Spaghetti
alla fornaia

THIS PASTA GETS ITS NAME — WHICH TRANSLATES AS 'BAKER'S SPAGHETTI' — FROM THE BREADCRUMBS RATHER THAN THE MORE UNUSUAL INGREDIENT, THE WALNUTS. ONCE COOKED OFF WITH THE GARLIC, THE WALNUTS DO LOSE A LITTLE OF THE WALNUTTINESS, BUT THEY DO PROVIDE A UNIQUE TEXTURE AND THAT IS WHAT THIS SAUCE IS ALL ABOUT. IT GOES WELL WITH STRONG WHITES SUCH AS PINOT GRIS AND LIGHTER BODIED REDS SUCH AS PINOT NOIR. **SERVES 4**

Ingredients

500 G (1 LB 2 OZ) spaghetti
100 G (3½ OZ / 1 CUP) walnuts
TWO CLOVES garlic
TWO TABLESPOONS virginal olive oil
50 G (1¾ OZ / ½ CUP) dry breadcrumbs
ONE TABLESPOON chopped flat-leaf (Italian) parsley

Method

Bring a large saucepan of well-salted water to a rolling boil and add the pasta. Meanwhile, chop up the nuts and garlic very finely. Heat a tablespoon of the olive oil in a frying pan and fry the walnuts, garlic and breadcrumbs until the garlic begins to change colour. Season to taste. When the pasta is cooked, drain and mix with the bread and walnut mixture and the remaining olive oil. Sprinkle with the parsley and serve.

Tumbet

ALTHOUGH IT MAY LOOK LIKE A THOUSAND OTHER BAKED EGGPLANT TYPE DISHES, THIS ONE TASTES QUITE DIFFERENT BECAUSE OF THE OLD SPANISH TECHNIQUES USED IN THE COOKING. IN SPAIN, TUMBET IS SERVED WITH FISH, MEAT OR EGGS, ON ITS OWN OR AT ROOM TEMPERATURE, AS TAPAS. IT GOES REALLY WELL WITH LIGHT REDS. **SERVES 4**

Ingredients

ONE large eggplant (aubergine)
500 G (1 LB 2 OZ) potatoes
ONE large green capsicum (pepper)
500 ML (17 FL OZ/2 CUPS) olive oil
1½ TINS (600 G/1 LB 5 OZ) whole tomatoes
THREE CLOVES garlic, crushed

Method

Cut the eggplant into 1 cm (½ in) slices and the peeled potatoes the same way. Seed and chop the capsicum in slightly thinner rings. Heat half the oil in a frying pan over medium heat and fry the potato slices until soft but not crisp or golden. Remove and layer the slices in a casserole dish. Fry the eggplant in the same oil until browned, then layer the eggplant on top of the potatoes. Next, fry the capsicum until soft and the skin is wrinkly. Place them on top of the eggplant and add some coarse salt. Open the tins of tomatoes and, with a knife, cut them into rough pieces in the tin. Fry the garlic cloves in the same oil until they start to turn golden, then add the tomatoes and cook for 10–15 minutes, stirring and breaking up the bigger bits of tomato until the oil starts to separate and come to the surface. Pour over the top of the eggplant mixture. Add what's left of the oil in the frying pan to the top. In a preheated 180°C (350°F/Gas 4) oven, bake for 30–45 minutes, until heated through and the eggplant is nice and mushy.

Tomates y aceite

THIS IS NOT SO MUCH A RECIPE AS A BREAKFAST SUGGESTION. THROW OUT THE SATURATED FATS AND GIVE IT A TRY. MY CONVERSION OCCURRED ON A SUNDAY MORNING IN A CAFÉ IN CORDOBA. I ASKED A NICE SPANISH LADY WHAT SHE WAS EATING FOR BREAKFAST AND SHE POLITELY GAVE ME SOME. BREAKFASTS HAVE NEVER BEEN THE SAME. **SERVES 1**

Ingredients

TWO ripe and tasty tomatoes
TWO SLICES crusty bread
A DRIZZLE of high-quality olive oil

Method

Dice the tomatoes, place them in a bowl and season with salt and pepper. Toast your bread and drizzle with a little olive oil. Place the tomatoes on top and prepare to be converted.

Crusty
linguine

HERE'S A PASTA WITH A TRADITIONAL BEGINNING — OLIVE OIL, ANCHOVIES, BLACK OLIVES AND BREADCRUMBS — BUT WITH A UNIQUE TWIST TO THE ENDING. IT'S CALABRIAN. CRUSTY LINGUINE GOES WELL WITH WINES THAT HAVE MINIMAL OR NO WOOD INFLUENCE — FULL-BODIED ACIDIC WHITES AND LIGHT, SLIGHTLY CHILLED REDS. **SERVES 4**

Ingredients

500 G (1 LB 2 OZ) linguine
250 ML (9 FL OZ/1 CUP) virginal olive oil
75 G (2½ OZ/½ CUP) chopped black olives
ONE dried chilli or small fresh one, seeded and finely chopped
ONE TABLESPOON capers
SIX anchovy fillets
40 G (1½ OZ/½ CUP) fresh breadcrumbs

Method

Boil a big saucepan of salted water and add the linguine, making sure no bits are stuck together (linguine has a habit of doing that). Heat half the olive oil in a saucepan and add the olives, chilli, capers and anchovies, and stir over medium heat until the anchovies have broken up and dissolved. Fry the breadcrumbs in a large non-stick frying pan with the rest of the oil until golden brown. When the linguine is cooked, mix in the anchovy and oil sauce and pour into the pan with the breadcrumbs. Fry the linguine in this pan over a medium–low heat until a crust has formed on the bottom. Invert onto a large plate, crusty side up, and cut into serving portions with a sharp knife.

Chapter 3
The Legume

Three common threads reach back into the rough fabric of early human history: poverty, the chickpea and the fart joke. All three are intrinsically linked: the chickpea was (and still is) an antidote to poverty, while flatulence is the direct result of chickpea consumption — especially when the peas haven't been soaked long enough. Fossilized chickpeas (they'd need a *lot* of soaking) have been discovered in both Italy and Switzerland, so it seems that even our Stone Age ancestors gassed each other with chickpeas. But the chickpea's big moment in history was no joke and it occurred relatively recently.

It was Easter Monday, March 31, 1282. Such was the moon cycle that Easter fell very early that year. Sicilians thronged in the church square at Palermo. They were waiting for the bells to ring for vespers to summon them inside to celebrate the resurrection of Christ. It was a time in Sicilian history when a Frenchman had become King of Sicily and the Sicilians weren't happy about it. In fact they hated it — as events will show. But I'll skip all the complicated dynastic, military and political events that led us to this point and get to the exciting bit.

The Sicilians were talking, gossiping and laughing, as people do on an Easter Monday holiday. Soon a group of drunken French soldiers began to join in the festivities and flirt with the younger Sicilian women. Among the French soldiers was a sergeant named Drouet, who was pestering a young woman and trying to drag her away from the rest of the crowd. This was going too far for her hot-blooded husband. He whipped a large carving knife from under his vest and plunged it into the sergeant's chest. The other French soldiers ran to Drouet's defence and soon found themselves encircled by a pack of knife-wielding Sicilians.

The timing was perfect. At the very moment when the blood was being spilled on the square, the bells of The Church of the Holy Spirit began to ring for vespers. To the pious Sicilians, the ringing bells was no coincidence; it was heavenly approbation for ridding Sicily of the accursed French soldiers. With the bells still ringing in their ears, the people ran through the streets calling for Sicilians to rid the town of the French. No French man, woman or child survived. Even Sicilian women married to Frenchmen died with their husbands. Often it was hard to tell who was French and who was Sicilian and when the rebels broke into the Dominican and Franciscan convents, they came up with an ingenious way to pick out the foreigners. The friars were dragged out and told to pronounce the word chickpea (*ceci* in Italian). It's a word that those brought up speaking French could never quite get right. That afternoon in Palermo, to mispronounce the word 'chickpea' meant death.

Despite this rather bloody association, the chickpea has always been considered a peaceful food, like the lentil. The lentil gets its name from the Latin word *lentus*, which means slow. The Romans thought that lentils encouraged a mildness of character. One Roman general even blamed a defeat on the fact that his army had eaten lentils pre-battle. Lentils were considered a 'cold' food, which calmed rather than excited. Because of this they were a favourite of parents for their children — an ancient cure for ADHD perhaps?

Besides its peaceful reputation, the lentil has always been a poor man's meat and it's true — 100 grams (3½ oz) of lentils gives you 25 grams (1 oz) of protein; while it takes 134 grams (4¾ oz) of beef to give you the same amount. This reputation has led to some terrible vegie food — the worst of which has to be the lentil burger.

As for the bean, it's older than the fart joke. The Asian soya bean has been traced back 4000 years, while the broad (fava) bean was already being cultivated in two separate varieties back in prehistoric times. But the bean that changed the world and European cooking forever is the relatively recent American haricot. The name comes from the Aztec word for bean (*ayacotli*), and is the ancestor of the borlotti (cranberry), cannellini and red kidney beans — as well as every other bean that is good in tins.

Before the discovery of the New World, Europe had a mono bean culture. There was the broad bean and that was pretty much it. But the situation was about to change via some powerful wealthy connections. In 1528, some New World haricots arrived on the desk of Pope Clement VII. The beans were delegated to Canon Pietro Valeriano in Florence to propagate. When he'd picked and cooked his first crop he declared them so good he gave some to Alessandro de Medici. Alessandro cooked and enjoyed them so much that when his daughter Catherine de Medici left for France in 1533 to marry Henry II, he put some beans in her saddlebags. Thus in one action, the bean was seeded into French cuisine and the curious custom of throwing food at newlyweds was born.

Medicinal
minestre

THIS ITALIAN SOUP GETS ITS NAME BECAUSE IT IS ALWAYS COOKED IN OUR HOUSEHOLD WHEN SOMEONE IS: A) CROOK, B) HUNGOVER, C) TIRED OF RESTAURANT FOOD, OR D) PREGNANT. IT HAS A SOOTHING QUALITY — JUST THE SMELL OF THE LENTILS COOKING WITH THE BAY LEAVES IS CURATIVE — AND IF YOU CHOOSE TO TAKE A MEDICINAL GLASS OF BASIC RED WINE, IT GOES WELL WITH THAT TOO. IT'S RELATED TO A FAMOUS MINESTRE FROM ABRUZZI CALLED 'MINESTRONE DELLE VIRTU' WHICH REPUTABLY RESTORES NOT ONLY HEALTH BUT VIRTUE. IF ONLY … **SERVES 4**

Ingredients

110 G (3¾ OZ/½ CUP) dried chickpeas, soaked overnight, or one tin (400 g/14 oz)
185 G (6½ OZ/1 CUP) brown lentils
FOUR bay leaves
THREE CLOVES garlic, crushed

THREE TABLESPOONS olive oil
ONE large onion
ONE celery stalk
THREE carrots
FOUR roma (plum) tomatoes, or one tin (400 g/14 oz)

Method

If using dried chickpeas, boil them until they are tender and drain. Put the lentils in a large saucepan with the chickpeas, bay leaves, garlic, 1.5 litres (52 fl oz/6 cups) water and a tablespoon of the olive oil. Bring to the boil and cook until the lentils are soft but still holding their shape. Meanwhile, chop the onion, slice the celery and dice the carrots. Heat the remaining olive oil in a frying pan and fry the chopped vegetables over medium heat for 7–8 minutes, or until the carrots start to soften. Chop the tomatoes and add to the mixture, stirring until they've broken up and the juice is released. Add this mixture to the lentil and chickpea brew and simmer for another 15 minutes. The lentils should be mushy and soupy in texture but still identifiable as lentils. Taste, season with salt and pepper and serve with crusty bread for dunking.

Garbanzo
hotpot

THIS IS AN ANCIENT SPANISH SOUP THAT YOU CAN STILL FIND ON THE ODD RESTAURANT MENU IN MADRID. ANCESTRAL HOTPOTS GO ALL THE WAY BACK TO ROMAN IBERIA. THE POTATO IN THIS PARTICULAR VERSION IS A LITTLE BIT OF AN ANACHRONISM — POTATOES HAVE ONLY BEEN IN SPAIN SINCE THE 16TH CENTURY. THIS SORT OF HOTPOT IS A FAVOURITE FOOD AT LENT BECAUSE IT IS SO FILLING. IT'S ALSO VERY HEALTHY. THE WATER IN WHICH THE SILVERBEET IS COOKED SERVES AS THE STOCK FOR THE SOUP. IT GOES WELL WITH LIGHTER STYLE RED WINES — INEXPENSIVE PINOT NOIR AND THAT SORT OF THING. **SERVES 4**

Ingredients

220 G (7¾ OZ/1 CUP) dried chickpeas, soaked overnight

ONE LARGE BUNCH silverbeet (Swiss chard), with the white bits removed, roughly chopped

500 G (1 LB 2 OZ) potatoes, cut into chunks

185 ML (6 FL OZ/¾ CUP) virginal olive oil

ONE THICK SLICE stale, hard Italian-style bread

TWO CLOVES garlic, cut into quarters

ONE onion, finely chopped

ONE TEASPOON Spanish smoked paprika (or standard paprika will do)

TWO hard-boiled eggs with yolks and whites separated

Method

Heat 2 litres (70 fl oz/8 cups) water in a large saucepan. When boiling, add the chickpeas, silverbeet, potatoes and a big pinch of salt, and cook slowly for an hour, or until the chickpeas are tender. Meanwhile, heat the oil in a frying pan and fry the bread till golden brown on both sides. Remove the bread and fry the garlic until golden. Remove the garlic and fry the onion in the same oil until it starts to brown, then add the paprika, stir, then add to the soup. Crush the garlic with the bread, egg yolks and a little salt in a mortar, then add to the soup along with the chopped egg white. Season if necessary and serve.

Mujaddara

THIS MIXTURE OF RICE AND LENTILS APPEARS IN MEDIEVAL COOKBOOKS, AND HISTORIANS SUGGEST THAT MUJADDARA MAY HAVE BEEN THE 'MESS OF POTAGE' REFERRED TO IN THE OLD TESTAMENT WITH WHICH TRICKY JACOB BOUGHT ESAU'S BIRTHRIGHT. THE NAME COMES FROM THE ARABIC WORD FOR SMALLPOX BECAUSE THE LENTILS IN THE RICE ARE SAID TO LOOK LIKE THE SCARRED FACE OF A SMALLPOX VICTIM — BUT DON'T LET THAT PUT YOU OFF. THIS IS THE SORT OF DISH THAT PREFERS A FAIRLY EARTHY CHEAP RED. **SERVES 4**

Ingredients

185 G (6½ OZ/1 CUP) brown lentils
TWO bay leaves
ONE CLOVE garlic, crushed
ONE TEASPOON cumin seeds
ONE TEASPOON coriander seeds
½ TEASPOON black peppercorns

THREE TABLESPOONS olive oil
FOUR brown onions: two finely chopped, two sliced into rings
200 G (7 OZ/1 CUP) long-grain rice
A KNOB of butter
thick yoghurt, to serve

Method

Rinse the lentils and put them in a large heavy-based saucepan with the bay leaves and crushed garlic. Pour in just enough water to cover and simmer until the lentils are tender, then drain. Meanwhile, in a small frying pan over low heat, roast the cumin and coriander seeds until fragrant, then pound in a mortar with the black peppercorns. Heat the olive oil in the saucepan you used for the lentils over medium heat and fry the chopped onions with the crushed spices until the onion browns. Stir in the lentils and rice with a couple of good pinches of salt and just enough water to cover. Bring the mixture to the boil and simmer until the rice has almost cooked and the water is almost gone.

Take the saucepan off the heat and cover the pan with a clean cloth and leave it to steam for another 15 minutes. Meanwhile, cook the sliced onions in butter (or olive oil if cholesterol is an issue) until they are browned and caramelized. Tip the rice and lentils into a serving dish, spoon the fried onions over the top and serve with thick, creamy yoghurt.

Fagioli al fiasco

DERIVED FROM AN ANTIQUE SOUP WHERE BEANS ARE SLOWLY COOKED WITH OLIVE OIL, SAGE AND GARLIC IN A POTTERY CHIANTI FLASK OVER A LOW FIRE, THIS TUSCAN MIXTURE IS ALSO CALLED 'LOMBARD SOUP' BECAUSE IT'S ATTRIBUTED TO ITINERANT LOMBARD VINEYARD WORKERS. THEY WOULD HAVE INVENTED IT MORE OUT OF NECESSITY THAN ANYTHING ELSE. NO ONE WOULD BELIEVE THAT SOMETHING SO SIMPLE COULD CREATE SOMETHING SO SATISFYING. IT SHOWS OFF A YOUNG FRUITY RED TO GREAT EFFECT AND LIKE MOST OF THE SOUPS IN THIS BOOK, CRUSTY BREAD IS A GIVEN. **SERVES 4**

Ingredients

200 G (7 OZ/1 CUP) dried cannellini beans, soaked overnight
SIX TABLESPOONS virginal olive oil
ONE BUNCH sage leaves
FOUR SLICES crusty Italian-style bread

Method

Put the cannellini beans in a saucepan with half the olive oil, the sage leaves, 1 litre (35 fl oz/4 cups) water and a big pinch of salt. Bring slowly to the boil, then simmer gently for about 3 hours, or until the beans are mushy but still holding their shape. When the soup is ready, adjust the seasoning. Toast the bread and put one slice into each dish (or two, if you're feeling hungry), drizzle with the remaining oil, sprinkle on some coarse salt and ladle the soupy beans on top.

Chole chaat

THIS IS A CHICKPEA CURRY THAT CAN BE SERVED AS A SIDE DISH TO A MEATIER MEAL OR ON ITS OWN AS VEGO, GLUTEN-FREE FARE. IF USING TINNED CHICKPEAS IT'S PROBABLY ONE OF THE FASTEST CURRIES OF THIS TYPE YOU CAN MAKE. AS WITH MOST SPICY FOOD, FRUITIER WINES WORK BETTER. THIS ONE GOES QUITE NICELY WITH A HEAVILY CHILLED ROSÉ. **SERVES 4**

Ingredients

220 G (7¾ OZ / 1 CUP) dried chickpeas, or two tins (800 g / 1 lb 12 oz)

TWO TABLESPOONS olive oil

ONE onion, diced

ONE TEASPOON ground cumin

ONE TEASPOON ground coriander

½ TEASPOON ground turmeric

ONE TIN (400 G / 14 OZ) tomatoes

½ A THUMB of ginger, finely chopped

TWO green chillies, finely chopped

Method

If using dried chickpeas soak them overnight and then boil in plenty of water until soft. This should take 1½–2 hours. Take half of the chickpeas and give them a whiz in a food processor or mash them with a potato masher.

Meanwhile, heat the oil in a heavy-based saucepan over medium heat. Sauté the onion, then add the dried spices and fry for a couple of minutes. Open the tin of tomatoes and chop them up in the tin with a knife. Add the ginger, chillies, tomatoes and their juice with a good pinch of salt, and stir. Finally mix in the mashed and unmashed chickpeas and simmer for about 15 minutes, or until the tomatoes are nicely broken up. Serve with basmati rice.

Lentil and
chorizo
risotto

THIS IS A BROWN LENTIL DISH WITH A RISOTTO TECHNIQUE. THIS VERSION USES CHORIZO BUT WORKS EQUALLY WELL WITH MEAT LEFTOVERS SUCH AS LAMB SHANKS, ROASTS, ETC, OR EVEN LEFTOVER BARBECUED SAUSAGES. **SERVES 4**

Ingredients

FOUR TABLESPOONS olive oil
ONE large onion, diced
TWO CLOVES garlic, finely chopped
185 G (6½ OZ/1 CUP) brown lentils
TWO chorizo sausages, chopped
1.25 LITRES (44 FL OZ/5 CUPS) Greg's quick chicken stock (page 73)
ONE LARGE HANDFUL flat-leaf (Italian) parsley, chopped

Method

Pour half the olive oil into a heavy-based saucepan over medium heat. Add the onion and garlic and fry until the onion is transparent, then add the lentils and stir for about 5 minutes. Add the chorizo and fry in the oil till the edges go crisp. Meanwhile, have the chicken stock simmering in another saucepan. Add the stock to the lentil pan and simmer, stirring occasionally. When the lentils are mushy and the consistency of thick porridge (it should take about 30 minutes) garnish with the parsley and serve.

Baked beans
the old way

RATHER THAN RIPPING THE LID OFF A TIN, THIS IS BAKED BEANS FOR THE PATIENT … OR PENITENT. IT WAS TRADITIONALLY PUT IN THE OVEN ON SATURDAY FOR CONSUMPTION ON RETURN FROM MASS ON SUNDAY. IF THAT DOESN'T FIT INTO YOUR HECTIC RELIGIOUS TIMETABLE, IT CAN BE READY IN 5 HOURS. **SERVES 4**

Ingredients

500 G (1 LB 2 OZ) dried cannellini or borlotti (fava) beans
TWO CLOVES garlic, chopped
ONE LARGE HANDFUL flat-leaf (Italian) parsley, chopped
SIX SLICES bacon

Method

Soak the beans overnight, then drain them and mix with the garlic and parsley. In an earthenware casserole dish, lay half the bacon on the bottom, pour in half the beans, then another layer of bacon, then the remaining beans. Season with freshly ground black pepper. Top with water so that it covers the beans by about 2 cm (¾ in). Cook very slowly until they're just mushy, checking the water level occasionally. The cooking time will depend on the oven and cooking vessel, but aim for about 5 hours at 120°C (235°F/Gas ½).

Chapter 4
The Squid

'You are what you eat.' If you take this old maxim too literally, you'd expect people to look like cows, pigs, sheep, fish, hydrolyzed vegetable protein or blocks of tofu. But then again … No, seriously, it is true that what humans have eaten over the centuries has had as much to do with what they aspire to be as to what they aspire to eat. Cannibals consumed their enemies to get their strength, and non-cannibals have eaten various things for the same reasons. The nobility always prized brave creatures over the less courageous — despite the fact that a wild boar might not taste half as good as a domesticated pig.

There are hundreds of examples of humans trying to digest virtues and attributes along with proteins and fats: the poor bull's testicles after the corrida, the tiger penis, the shark fin — but in all this, the poor old cephalopod doesn't get a look in — the squid has never been eaten for those reasons.

While eight arms might be useful and the ability to squirt ink in the faces of those you fear would come in handy, there aren't too many who hanker for the look or behaviour of the squid. Some exhibit the squid-like attributes of voracious appetite and predatory sexual behaviour but this probably has nothing to do with calamari consumption. Where the squid is concerned, as with everything, it all comes down to looks and whichever way you look at it — apart from on a plate in pretty little rings — the squid is an ugly thing. That's what's kept the price down.

According to current classification there are 786 species of cephalopods, of which 298 are squid and 289 are octopuses. The variety of squid commercially caught in Australia is known as gould's squid, the arrow squid, or more properly as *Nototodarus gouldi*. They grow incredibly fast. Gould's squid reaches full size in 18 months and females grow up to 4 centimetres (1½ in) a month. That means they are eternally hungry, which helps in the catching. Squid fishing is done in the night. The boat shines bright lights into the water that attract sundry little fish. The squid hides in the shadows of the boat and darts out to catch its prey and gets caught in turn.

The squid's insatiable appetite, tendency towards cannibalism and propensity to take sexual favours by force are well documented, but an interesting cephalopod characteristic was discovered quite recently. All squid are not the same. Squid have personalities: some are shy, some are bullies and some squid are trickier than others. It seems that about 30 per cent of a squid's 'personality' is passed on to their offspring. If you think this sounds a little far-fetched consider this: relative to their size, squid have brains the size of a cat's. If that makes them a little less attractive as food, there is a positive. The squid's speedy lifecycle means it's seafood you can eat without fear of heavy metals or guilt — it's one of the few fisheries at present that is sustainable.

The whole squid fishing industry is relatively new in Australia. The Japanese and Koreans were fishing for squid in Australia's southern oceans for ages before Australians got interested. Australians still catch only 2000 tonnes and import 11,000 tonnes — most of which ends up deep-fried as calamari rings in fish and chip shops and in clubs and pubs.

The squid is yet to find a place in our kitchen culture. That's why I'm devoting a chapter to it. I'd like to see the squid tube hold the same place in our hearts and fridges as the lamb chop or T-bone steak. For the creative, cash-strapped cook this ugly, intelligent cephalopod is a boon — a blank canvas that absorbs flavours like a sponge. That weird piece of strangely rubbery seafood can be stuffed, curled, curried, stir-fried, barbecued … there isn't much you can't do with the mantle of a squid if you put your mind to it.

● ● ● ● ● ● ● ● ● ● ● ● ●

Yaki squid

THIS IS THE JAPANESE VERSION OF CALAMARI AND IS BEST SERVED AS A STARTER. TYPICALLY NIPPON, IT IS FRESH, LIGHT AND HEALTHFUL TASTING AND GOES VERY WELL WITH AROMATIC WHITE WINES SUCH AS LIMEY, YOUNG RIESLINGS AND SEMILLON SAUVIGNON BLANC BLENDS. IT REQUIRES VERY FRESH SQUID. **SERVES 4**

Ingredients

TWO small squid tubes
A DRIZZLE of olive oil
TWO spring onions (scallions), finely chopped
ONE TABLESPOON freshly grated ginger
A DRIZZLE of light soy sauce

Method

Heat up the grill-plate part of a barbecue as high as it goes. The aim of this is to get crisscross burn marks on the squid. Rinse the squid inside and out and, for extra scorching, brush the outside with a little olive oil. Put the squid tubes on the barbie and cook for 4–5 minutes on each side, then remove them. Don't turn it too soon or you won't get the pretty burn marks. Holding the hot tubes with tongs, cut the squid into 2 mm ($^1/_{16}$ in) rings with a sharp knife. You want them to be a bit thinner than standard calamari. Serve topped with the spring onions, grated ginger and a drizzle of light soy sauce.

Squid and silverbeet stir-fry

HERE IS A RECIPE BORN OUT OF NECESSITY WHEN THERE WAS NOTHING IN THE HOUSE BUT SOME FRESH RICE NOODLES, A FROZEN SQUID TUBE AND SOME SILVERBEET (SWISS CHARD). IT GIVES THE STANDARD STIR-FRY A BIT OF A DIFFERENT SLANT AND A WHOLE LOT MORE IRON. **SERVES 4**

Ingredients

TWO small squid tubes

TWO CLOVES garlic

ONE THUMB of ginger

ONE large onion

ONE large red or green chilli

1½ TABLESPOONS oil

ONE TABLESPOON sweet chilli sauce

ONE TABLESPOON fish sauce

ONE TABLESPOON soy sauce

ONE BUNCH silverbeet (Swiss chard), with the white bits removed

TWO SMALL PACKETS fresh rice noodles

ONE HANDFUL peanuts (optional)

ONE SMALL HANDFUL coriander (cilantro) leaves, chopped

Method

To make those pretty, curled squid rings, cut the squid tubes along the side and lay them flat on a chopping board. Using a sharp knife, score the inside with diagonal slashes, being careful not to cut right through. Slice into 2 cm (¾ in) strips and chop those strips in half. Finely chop the garlic and ginger, slice the onion and chilli. Put a tablespoon of oil in your wok or frying pan and stir-fry all those ingredients until the garlic begins to go golden. Add the squid and stir-fry over high heat until it curls and starts to brown, then pour in the sauces and then add the silverbeet. Fry for a couple of minutes until the silverbeet is well wilted and cooked through. Stir in the rice noodles, the peanuts (if using) and mix over the heat for another minute or so. Add the coriander and serve.

Curried
squid

A CURRIED SQUID DISH LIKE THIS ONE IS HANDY IN THAT IT CAN CAMOUFLAGE A SQUID THAT IS FROZEN OR NOT QUITE FRESH. THE SQUID TUBES SOLD IN MOST FISH SHOPS ARE FROM DISTANT LANDS AND ARE PERFECT FOR THIS SORT OF CURRIED DISGUISE. THE MIX OF SPICES AND SILKY FEEL OF THIS CURRY GIVES IT A LUXURIOUS NATURE AND IT GOES WELL WITH WHITE WINE WITH AN UNCTUOUS TEXTURE — PINOT GRIS OR VIOGNIER. **SERVES 4**

Ingredients

700 G (1 LB 9 OZ) squid tubes
ONE TEASPOON cumin seeds
ONE TEASPOON coriander seeds
ONE small dried chilli
1/2 TEASPOON ground turmeric
TWO TABLESPOONS olive oil
ONE onion, finely chopped

TEN curry leaves
ONE THUMB of ginger, finely chopped
FOUR CLOVES garlic, finely chopped
170 ML (5 1/2 FL OZ/2/3 CUP) coconut milk
ONE lime, juiced

Method

Rinse the tubes and cut them into 2 cm (3/4 in) rings. In a small frying pan over low heat, roast the cumin and coriander until fragrant. Grind both in a mortar with the chilli and turmeric. Coat the squid rings in this powder.

Heat the olive oil in a heavy-based frying pan and fry the onion until browned. Add the curry leaves, ginger and garlic and fry for a bit longer. Pour in the coconut milk and bring to the boil. Throw in the squid rings and stir. Simmer for 4–5 minutes, or until the squid is tender. Stir in the lime juice at the last moment and serve with jasmine rice.

Calamares

THERE ARE AS MANY VERSIONS FOR FRIED SQUID AS THERE ARE FOR THE POTATO CHIP. THIS IS THE ONE YOU FIND IN ANDALUCIA. ALTHOUGH IT LOOKS LIKE FRIED SQUID RINGS, THE REAL CALAMARES ARE QUITE DIFFERENT TO THE ONES YOU FIND IN RSL CLUBS — AND IT'S SERVED WITH PROPER MAYO. IT'S A FISH DISH THAT WILL GO HAPPILY WITH A GLASS OF CHILLED WHITE (BUT NOTHING TOO OAKY), CHILLED LIGHT RED OR A COLD LAGER. **SERVES 4**

Ingredients

TWO squid tubes
ONE lemon, juiced
TWO CLOVES garlic, crushed
plain (all-purpose) flour, enough to coat the squid
ONE egg, beaten
dry breadcrumbs, enough to coat the squid
olive oil, for frying
proper mayo (page 35), to serve

Method

Cut the squid tubes into rings and marinate in a mixture of lemon juice and crushed garlic overnight. Put the flour in a plastic bag, followed by the squid rings and give them a good shake to coat them in the flour. Dunk them in the beaten egg and then in the breadcrumbs. Fry in hot olive oil quickly — 20–30 seconds each side should be enough — and drain on paper towels. Serve hot with proper mayo on the side.

Squid and
beans

SQUID AND BEANS IS AN UNLIKELY COMBO BUT THE RESULTS OF THIS MARRIAGE ARE SURPRISINGLY HARMONIOUS. INVENTED BY THE LANDLOCKED NON-SEAFOOD-EATING FLORENTINES, IT'S THE SORT OF FOOD THAT WILL BE ENJOYED BY THOSE WHO DON'T USUALLY ORDER SQUID FROM A MENU. THE BEAN, SAGE AND TOMATO BASE MAKE IT FISH FOR RED WINE. IT GOES VERY WELL WITH BUDGET PINOT NOIR. **SERVES 4**

Ingredients

200 G (7 OZ/1 CUP) dried cannellini beans
FOUR TABLESPOONS virginal olive oil
ONE BUNCH sage leaves
500 G (1 LB 2 OZ) small squid, cleaned and cut into rings
TWO CLOVES garlic, crushed
ONE TIN (400 G/14 OZ) tomatoes

Method

Soak the beans overnight. Drain them and put them in a heavy-based saucepan with 2 tablespoons of olive oil and about a dozen or so sage leaves. Add water to cover the beans and slowly bring to the boil, then simmer gently for 1½–2 hours, or until the beans are tender and the mixture is thick. When the beans are done, heat the remaining olive oil in a frying pan and throw in the squid rings and crushed garlic. Fry over medium heat for about 5 minutes, being careful not to burn the garlic. Add the tinned tomatoes and cook until the tomatoes have broken up and the juice has reduced a little. Pour the contents of the frying pan into the bean mixture and heat for a further 5–10 minutes. Season with salt and pepper and serve.

Calamari ripieni al Gregorini

A SQUID HOOD IS BASICALLY A SEAFOOD FLAVOURED SAUSAGE CASING TO BE FILLED WITH WHATEVER YOUR IMAGINATION IMAGINES. MY STUFFED SQUID DISH TAKES A LITTLE FROM ITALIAN AND GREEK VERSIONS AND HAS AN ANDALUCIAN INFLUENCE AS WELL. IT MAKES A GOOD STARTER OR LUNCHEON REPAST AND GOES NICELY WITH LIGHT REDS. **SERVES 4**

Ingredients

FOUR baby squid

TWO onions

FOUR CLOVES garlic

TWO TABLESPOONS olive oil

220 G (7³/4 OZ/1 CUP) arborio rice

TWO TINS (800 G/1 LB 12 OZ) tomatoes

Greg's quick chicken stock (page 73), boiling

ONE LARGE HANDFUL mixed basil, flat-leaf (Italian) parsley and coriander (cilantro) leaves

FOUR TABLESPOONS dry white wine

Method

First of all clean the squid: take out the quill, guts and skin and discard. Cut off the tentacles and wings, chop them finely and put aside. Rinse the tube in water. Dice 1 onion, finely chop 2 garlic cloves and sauté them in a tablespoon of olive oil in a large heavy-based saucepan over low heat until the onion is transparent. Add the rice and the chopped tentacles and wings and stir them into the oil and onion mixture as if you were making a risotto. When the rice has lost its chalky colour and absorbed the oil, add half a tin of tomatoes, a little bit of chicken stock, the herbs and a good splash of dry white wine. Keep cooking as you would a risotto: adding chicken stock as required, and stirring for about another 8 minutes. Take it off the heat. When it has cooled down enough to handle, spoon the mixture into each of the squid tubes, making sure that each one has a bit of tomato in it — the juices from the tomato will help cook the rice. Don't over-pack the squid or the rice will come out the ends as the rice expands. Close the tubes with a toothpick threaded through the opening.

Now for the sauce. Dice the other onion and finely chop the remaining garlic. Fry together with the remaining olive oil in the same saucepan over low heat until the onion is transparent. Add the rest of the tomatoes and a splash of white wine, a couple of good pinches of salt and some cracked black pepper. Simmer for about 5 minutes, or until the tomatoes are nicely broken up. Lay the stuffed squid in the sauce so that they are mostly submerged. Simmer gently in the sauce, turning them occasionally for about another 20 minutes. Take the squid from the pan, cut them into slices and pour the sauce over the top. Serve with a green salad and crusty bread.

Chapter 5
The Chicken

When God saw how man struggled after being thrown out of the Garden of Eden he took pity and created a bird. This was a bird that could not fly and could not even run very fast. It laid an egg every day, survived on scraps and seed and had tasty white flesh. But as one last reminder of the 'fall', God made the male of the species sing relentlessly at dawn to awaken man once more to the plough and hoe.

Actually this didn't happen at all. Like most animals in this book, the chook is a human creation — created by selective breeding. When the chicken first appears in history, it's in India 4000 years ago and it wasn't a chicken for eating. It was *Gallus gallus*, the original Red Rooster — a small, rusty-coloured jungle fowl domesticated for use in religious ceremonies. Somehow in the sacrifice and burning of the offerings, the savour of roasting chicken was too much to resist and the jungle chook charmed its way from altar to table.

From there it became *Gallus gallus domesticus* and spread everywhere man did. The Romans especially loved the chook. Marcus Gavius Apicius, a Roman who lived during the reign of Tiberius, wrote one of the earliest surviving cookbooks. It is a cookbook surprisingly similar to this one. There's a chapter on the cooking of quadrupeds, the obligatory lentil, chickpea and bean chapter and two chapters on poultry, including some 17 recipes for chook. Unfortunately most of them aren't very good.

But it wasn't just at the table that the chicken was prized. As with other birds, the Romans believed that the behaviour of a chook could foretell events. The chicken went under the same prognostic guidelines that applied for crows and owls. If a chicken was spotted flying over your left shoulder everything would be okay — the gods were on your side. As chickens don't fly very well, this probably didn't happen very often. Another method of observing chicken behaviour was invented — auspicium ex tripudiis. *This entailed feeding the chooks and noting if they ate or not. If they ate hungrily all was well, but if they made noises, beat their wings and did anything else that poultry do — bad things would happen.*

There's a story related by Suetonius about an old relation of Tiberius, Publius Claudius Pulcher, who consulted his soothsaying chooks before an important naval battle off the coast of Sicily. No matter what he did, the chooks refused to eat. Angry, he threw them overboard saying, 'If they will not eat, let them drink'. The chooks were right. He lost the battle and was later tried for impiety.

Interestingly, the Roman senate was forever passing laws against the overfeeding of chickens. The Roman palate adored roast chooks that were overfed on bread soaked in milk. Those same overfed chooks, when it came time to predict the future, probably wouldn't eat. Ipso facto lots of bad things kept happening. The question begs: were overfed chooks the reason for the fall of the Roman Empire?

The savour of roast chicken does strange things to people. Saint Thomas Aquinas, a medieval mind of the highest order, used his finely honed dialectic skills to try and get it back on the menu on fast days. It had been forbidden since the Council of Aachen in 817 as being far too sumptuous for Fridays. Thomas cleverly argued that the chicken was of aquatic origin and thereby edible on fast days under the same terms as fish. He prevailed, but was later overruled.

Until recently, roasting a chicken represented material comfort. Henry Navarre in the 16th century came to the throne making promises like a modern politician. He declared he would put a chicken in every peasant's pot on Sundays. He didn't. It wasn't a core promise.

Chicken has only become commonplace in Australia relatively recently. In the 1960s it wasn't on the menu. When the Beatles came to Australia in 1964, the average Australian was eating 4.9 kilos (10 lb 13 oz) of chicken per year. In 1974 Australians were eating 13.4 kilos (29 lb 9 oz) and by 2004 the figure was 32.8 kilos (72 lb 5 oz). That's about 20 chooks per person per year. But they're rarely eaten as entire birds complete with neck and giblets. We consume chicken as components: breasts, thighs, legs, wings, necks, livers, burgers, sausages …

Chicken has changed, and from a cook's point of view a tender roast chicken is no longer a challenge. They're not the old broilers our ancestors had to deal with; but they are tasteless — at least the average Australian supermarket chicken is. Chicken culture is different throughout the world. In France, a supermarket-bought chook is a cornfed, scrawny little number with yellow skin and flesh. But they taste so chickeny it's as if they're on flavour enhancers. In Australia, chicken producers seem to think that we like them fat and tasteless. The best advice is buy them on the lean side and if you're roasting them, make sure they're free range.

● ● ● ● ● ● ● ● ● ● ● ● ●

Greg's quick chicken stock

THIS IS AN EASY STOCK YOU CAN USE AS CHICKEN SOUP (JUST ADD NOODLES) OR STRAIN TO MAKE AN EXCELLENT STOCK. **MAKES 2 LITRES (70 FL OZ/8 CUPS)**

Ingredients

ONE chicken drumstick
ONE onion, diced
ONE BUNCH celery, tops and leaves only
THREE CLOVES garlic, crushed

Method

Put all the ingredients in a large saucepan over medium–high heat with 2 litres (70 fl oz/8 cups) cold water. Add 2 big pinches of salt and 4 or 5 good grinds of black pepper. When it comes to the boil, reduce the heat and simmer until the meat on the leg is coming off the bone. If using as a soup, take the meat off the bone, remove the celery and serve. If using as a stock, strain and refrigerate or freeze for later use.

Thai-died
chicken

HERE'S A METHOD OF COOKING CHOOK THAT ONCE LEARNED OFF BY HEART WILL BECOME A BARBECUE STAPLE. HARDER TO RUIN THAN IT IS TO COOK, EVEN THE MOST BOOF-HEADED BARBECUER WON'T STUFF IT UP. THE PEPPER, GARLIC AND SCORCH FACTOR MEAN THAT THIS IS WHITE MEAT FOR RED WINE. GO FOR A LIGHT PEPPERY SHIRAZ FROM A COOLER CLIMATE AND THE PIQUANCY OF THE CHICKEN WILL PICK UP THE SPICINESS OF THE WINE. **SERVES 4**

Ingredients

1 KG (2 LB 4 OZ) fresh chicken pieces: thighs and drumsticks, or thigh fillets
TWO TABLESPOONS black peppercorns
SIX OR SEVEN CLOVES garlic
ONE LARGE HANDFUL coriander (cilantro) roots, stems and leaves, chopped
ONE TABLESPOON white wine
ONE TABLESPOON olive oil

Method

Clean the fatty bits off the chook pieces and prick them all over with a fork. Pound the pepper in a mortar to a coarse powder, then add the garlic, coriander and 2 teaspoons coarse salt. Pound into mush and use the wine to make a paste. Add the oil last and mix into a lotion that can be rubbed all over the chook. Marinate for a few hours — the longer the better. Cook on the grill of a hot barbecue until nicely browned and cooked through. Serve with rice.

Pollo fritto

THIS IS A TASTY, EASY, WINE-FRIENDLY WAY TO MAKE FRIED CHOOK. THE MAGIC INGREDIENT IS THE LEMON. IT PROVIDES A CLEANSING BACKGROUND TO THE FRIED FLAVOURS, AND WHEN SERVED WITH A SIMPLE GREEN SALAD AND A GLASS OF PINOT GRIGIO THE EFFECT IS MUCH LIGHTER THAN ONE IMAGINES FRIED CHOOK COULD BE. **SERVES 4**

Ingredients

1 KG (2 LB 4 OZ) chicken thighs
THREE TABLESPOONS olive oil
TWO TABLESPOONS lemon juice
ONE TEASPOON lemon zest
olive oil, for frying
plain (all-purpose) flour, for coating the chicken

Method

Give the thighs a bit of a bash with a meat mallet to make them more or less the same thickness. Combine the olive oil, lemon juice, lemon zest and a teaspoon each of salt and pepper and marinate the chicken in this for at least a couple of hours. Heat enough oil in a large frying pan to come halfway up the sides of the chicken pieces. Meanwhile, dust the chicken in flour. You can dunk them in beaten egg first though this is not entirely necessary. When the oil is at frying temperature — a piece of bread dropped in the oil should brown in 15 seconds — place the chicken in the oil, being careful not to crowd the pan. When one side is golden brown turn it over. The process should take about 4 minutes per side depending on the size of the thighs. There is nothing worse than raw chook so err on the side of well-cooked. When you can stick a skewer in the chicken and the juices run clear it's usually okay. Rest the chicken pieces on paper towel. Serve with a salad of green leaves.

Gallina en pepitoria

THIS CHOOK DISH DATES BACK TO SPAIN'S GOLDEN AGE WHEN PHILIP II RULED AND ALL THE RICHES FROM THE NEW WORLD WERE SHIPPED BACK TO SPAIN. ALAS PHILIP DIED, THE GOLD RAN OUT, THE ARMADA SANK AND SPAIN'S GLORIOUS AGE CAME TO A GRINDING HALT. HOWEVER, IT STILL EXISTS IN THIS DISH. THIS RECIPE HAS SURVIVED IN VARIOUS ANCIENT COOKBOOKS, INCLUDING THE 17TH CENTURY FOLIO FROM WHICH THIS VERSION DERIVES. NO DOUBT WITH BREEDING PROGRAMS, HORMONES AND ALL THE OTHER EVILS, THE CHOOK HAS EVOLVED A BIT SINCE THE 1600S BUT TRY TO FIND AN OLD-FASHIONED BIRD. **SERVES 4**

Ingredients

FOUR TABLESPOONS olive oil
ONE THICK SLICE crusty bread
TWELVE almonds, skin on
THREE CLOVES garlic
ONE chicken, cut into pieces

ONE large onion, finely chopped
ONE lemon, juiced
TWO hard-boiled egg yolks
1/2 TEASPOON cumin seeds

Method

Heat the oil in a large frying pan or flameproof casserole dish and fry the bread until golden along with the almonds and garlic. Remove and set aside. Fry the chicken gently in the same oil until the skin browns, then remove. Fry the onion in the same oil until soft. Return the chicken back to the pan along with the lemon juice and enough water (about 500 ml/17 fl oz/2 cups) to cover, and simmer over low heat for about 1 hour, or until the chicken is coming off the bone. Meanwhile, put the fried bread, almonds, garlic, egg yolks and cumin seeds in a mortar along with a little of the liquid from the chicken and pound into a mush. Add this mush to the chicken and simmer very gently for a further 10 minutes, or until the sauce thickens. Serve with rice and green vegetables.

Empadas de galinha

THE INSPIRATION FOR THESE CHICKEN PIES COMES FROM THE PORTUGUESE PROVINCE OF ALENTEJO. THESE PIES MAKE EXCELLENT PICNIC OR PARTY FOOD AND IF YOU USE SUPERMARKET FROZEN PUFF PASTRY THEY'RE DEAD EASY. THEY GO NICELY WITH INEXPENSIVE PINOT NOIRS. **MAKES 20–24 PIES**

Ingredients

1 KG (2 LB 4 OZ) chicken drumsticks

TWO chorizo sausages

ONE onion

FOUR SLICES bacon

ONE SMALL BUNCH flat-leaf (Italian) parsley, tied together

100 ML (3½ FL OZ) riesling

100 ML (3½ FL OZ) white wine vinegar

FOUR egg yolks

ONE lemon, juiced

frozen puff pastry

Method

Put the drumsticks into a large saucepan with the chorizo, onion, bacon and parsley. Pour on the riesling and the vinegar, then cover with water. Bring to the boil and simmer for about 1 hour, or until the chicken meat is falling off the bone. Take the pan off the heat and set aside the drumsticks, chorizo and bacon. Discard the parsley and onion. Put the liquid back on the stove and simmer until it starts to thicken, then remove from the stove and allow to cool. With your fingers, shred the chicken from the bone, throwing out the cartilage, skin and bone. Cut the chorizos into slices and halve them. Dice the bacon.

Now for the sauce. Once the liquid has cooled to lukewarm, stir in 3 of the egg yolks and heat very slowly, stirring all the time, until the sauce thickens. Add the lemon juice and a few grinds of black pepper, test for salt and then pour the sauce over the meat and mix together.

Lay the pastry out in sheets and, with a pie cutter or cup, cut out circles of pastry. Lay them in a greased muffin tin or similar, fill with the chicken mixture, put the pastry on top and brush with the remaining beaten egg yolk. Cook in a preheated 200°C (400°F/Gas 6) oven for about 30 minutes, or until the pastry browns. These pies can be frozen and reheated quite successfully.

Frango recheado a antiga moda Portugesa

THE TITLE OF THIS ROAST CHOOK TRANSLATES AS 'STUFFED CHICKEN THE OLD PORTUGUESE WAY'. IT HARKS BACK TO A TIME WHEN POOR PEOPLE ONLY ATE CHICKEN WHEN AN OLD FOWL'S LAYING DAYS WERE OVER. THOSE OLD LAYERS WERE TOUGH BIRDS AND IT WASN'T JUST A MATTER OF WHACKING THEM IN THE OVEN AND TURNING UP THE HEAT. A LITTLE PREP WAS REQUIRED IF THE FLESH WAS TO BE MASTICATE-ABLE. OFTEN, AS IS THE CASE HERE, THE CHOOK WAS ALSO USED AS A BAKING RECEPTACLE FOR OTHER TASTY VIANDS. THE MODERN CHICKEN IS A VERY DIFFERENT BIRD, BUT THIS DISH IS STILL A HANDY WAY TO MAKE A NUMBER 19 CHOOK A BIT MORE INTERESTING. WITH ALL THESE OTHER FLAVOURS GOING ON, IT ALSO MEANS THAT DRINKING SHIRAZ IS NOT OUT OF THE QUESTION. **SERVES 4**

Ingredients

TWO CLOVES garlic, finely chopped
ONE TABLESPOON paprika
FOUR TABLESPOONS olive oil
125 ML (4 FL OZ/^{1}/$_2$ CUP) red wine
ONE big chicken

STUFFING
ONE onion, finely chopped
TWO CLOVES garlic, finely chopped
ONE TABLESPOON olive oil
250 G (9 OZ) minced (ground) pork

100 G (3^1/$_2$ OZ/1 CUP) coarse dry
breadcrumbs
ONE hard-boiled egg, chopped
220 G (7^3/$_4$ OZ/^{1}/$_3$ CUP) chopped,
pitted green olives
ONE SMALL HANDFUL flat-leaf (Italian)
parsley, chopped
ONE TABLESPOON paprika
125 ML (4 FL OZ/^{1}/$_2$ CUP) unwooded
white wine

Method

Plan ahead. This is a dish for tomorrow not for today. Combine the garlic, 1 teaspoon coarse salt, paprika, oil and red wine and rub all over the bird, inside and out. Cover and refrigerate overnight. Now for the stuffing. In a frying pan over low heat, gently sauté the chopped onion and garlic in the olive oil until lightly golden. Add the pork and stir to break up the chunks for a few minutes, then cover with a lid and steam for about 20 minutes. Meanwhile, mix the breadcrumbs, egg, olives, parsley, 1 teaspoon ground black pepper and paprika in a large bowl. When the pork is cooked mix this in too. Add some white wine to moisten the mixture but don't make it wet. Stuff as much as you can into the cavity of the chicken and skewer the cloaca shut.

Rub the marinated chicken with a little bit more oil and place, breast side up, in a roasting tin in a 220°C (425°F/Gas 7) oven for 20 minutes. Turn the oven down to 180°C (350°F/Gas 4) and roast for another hour, or until the drumsticks move in their sockets. Remove the stuffing and serve in a separate dish, and carve the bird. Serve with plenty of greens.

Chapter 6
The Pig

Pigs are controversial. Loved, loathed and outlawed, a pork dish can still cause embarrassment at a modern, liberated dinner party. The porcine is a world full of paradoxes. Consider this one: pig is the world's leading source of meat yet Judaism and Islam, two of the world's most populous religions, ban it.

Depending on your deity, the pig seems to be a gift from God — so perfectly is it designed for human consumption. But God can't take the credit. It seems that there was never a wild pig, as such — although this is still a question of debate. Historians speculate that the pig we consume today was bred from domesticated wild boars so long ago that the link between the two species has long since disappeared.

Doubtless, the pig has been a part of human existence since the beginning of human existence and for a number of very good reasons. It is the epitome of fecundity. Excepting the rabbit, it is the most prolific breeder of domesticated animals. A pig farmer with a bit of time on his hands once sat down with pen and paper and worked out that in 12 years a single sow could produce over six million descendents!

Pork is also cheap meat to produce. Pigs eat anything. They are one of the most efficient converters of carbohydrates to proteins and fats. A cow needs three times as much food to produce as much meat and cows don't eat scraps. It's not surprising then that pork was almost the only meat eaten by European peasants for more than 2000 years. It has only been religious embargos that have stopped porcine world domination.

But if you study the religious injunctions against pork it quickly becomes apparent that the reason pork is banned is not very clear. Most think the reason is preservation — or spoilage. Yet pork is one of the easiest meats to preserve. It can be salted, smoked, air-dried, preserved in its own fat, doused in chemicals — there are numerous ways to stop a pig carcass going off. So why is it banned?

The passage concerning pork occurs in The Old Testament in Leviticus Chapter 11 in the Third Book of Moses. And God didn't ban just pork, either. The Lord told Moses and the Children of Israel that they couldn't eat: camels, rabbits, anything in the sea that wasn't a fish, eagles, owls, cuckoos, swans, pelicans, storks, herons, ferrets, mice, tortoises, lizards, snails, moles, snakes and all 'flying creeping things', except locusts and beetles.

The reason the pig was biblically banned has more to do with mobilization than preservation. The Hebrews were nomadic sheep herders and pigs, no matter how hard you try, won't herd. They run off squealing in separate directions. Raising pigs means staying in the same spot. Pigs equal urbanization and back in Moses' time, that wasn't an option for the Children of Israel.

Delve a little deeper into history and you discover that the prejudice against the pig goes well beyond the Hebrews. Even the Egyptians, according to Herodotus, regarded the swine as 'unclean' (though they still farmed and ate it); and like many reasonless superstitions, suspicion of pork still exists today — even among atheist and agnostic meat eaters.

The window of your average suburban butcher shop reveals the suspicion with which we still view the pig. Tucked down one end you'll find a pork roast, a few chops, some sausages and a loin roast — if you're lucky. But that's a lot more pork than there used to be. Australians have dismounted from the sheep's back and taken to riding the pig. We now eat more pork than lamb. We're still not eating trotters, heads and the other bits and pieces that Mediterranean Europeans love; and we still don't know how to cook it. Superstitious fears lurk in our hearts and more often than not we feel a religious injunction to cook the bejesus out of it. Fortunately, many cuts of pork can handle this abuse.

Pork is ambiguous meat. White or red? Lean or fatty? It is both and this ambiguity is a boon and a challenge. Lean pork is a blank canvas, smoked pork is like nothing else on the planet, and fatty pork reacts with red wine tannins in a most gustatory way. Drink the right wine with the right pork dish and it can taste Godly. But getting the wine right doesn't come as intuitively as it does with, say, a piece of fish or a lamb chop. Practice makes perfect. Experimentation is what it's all about. Here are a few wine-friendly recipes from different cuts of pork that won't cost an arm and a leg.

Ribs, peppers and potato curry

WE HAVE COLUMBUS TO THANK FOR CAPSICUMS AND FOR THEIR MISNOMER, PEPPERS. WHEN COLUMBUS ATE THE FOOD OF SOUTH AMERICA HE MISTOOK THE FLAVOUR OF CHILLI FOR PEPPER. ONCE 'PEPPERS' WERE IN THE POT WITH PORK, THEIR SPECIAL COMBINATION SOON BECAME OBVIOUS. THERE ARE NOW HUNDREDS OF RECIPES FROM MANY COUNTRIES THAT USE THAT MIX OF PORK AND PEPPER. THIS ONE IS QUITE A COMPLEX LITTLE NUMBER, BOTH IN ITS FLAVOURS AND ITS COOKING — BUT IT IS WORTH THE EFFORT. IT'S QUITE SPICY SO DON'T WASTE YOUR BEST REDS ON IT. **SERVES 4**

Ingredients

HALF a green capsicum (pepper)
HALF a red capsicum (pepper)
125 ML (4 FL OZ/¹/₂ CUP) olive oil
FOUR CLOVES garlic, finely chopped
ONE large onion, finely chopped
ONE THUMB of ginger, finely chopped
FOUR bay leaves
500 G (1 LB 2 OZ) boneless pork
spare ribs
ONE TABLESPOON coriander seeds

ONE TABLESPOON cumin seeds
¹/₂ TEASPOON ground turmeric
¹/₂ TEASPOON garam masala
ONE lemon
FOUR dried chillies
ONE TEASPOON mustard seeds
THREE ripe tomatoes, chopped
1¹/₂ TEASPOONS paprika
500 G (1 LB 2 OZ) potatoes (sebagos
are good), cubed

Method

Slice the capsicums into 1 cm (¹/₂ in) strips, then cut each strip in half. Heat half the oil in a flameproof casserole dish over medium heat and add half of the garlic, onion and ginger and all of the bay leaves, and fry until the onion softens. Increase the heat to high, add the pork to the dish and brown, then reduce the heat to medium again and cook for 10 minutes or so. Remove to a large bowl. Meanwhile, in a small frying pan, roast the coriander and cumin seeds and pound to a powder in a mortar. Mix half the coriander and cumin with the turmeric and garam masala and coat the meat with it. Finally, squeeze the lemon over the meat.

Heat the remaining oil in the casserole dish and fry the remaining onion, garlic and ginger until the onion is transparent. Add the dried chillies, mustard seeds and remaining coriander and cumin. Fry until the mustard seeds start to pop. Add the tomatoes and fry over medium heat until the tomatoes have broken up. Add the meat, paprika and capsicum and stir the mixture over medium heat. Pour in a little water to keep the mixture simmering and not sticking. Simmer for 15 minutes, then add the cubed sebagos and enough water to cover and simmer with the lid on for another 15 minutes, or until the potatoes are soft and have thickened up the sauce and the pork is tender. Serve with basmati rice.

Pork steaks
and wine-infused cabbage

THIS RECIPE IS CREDITED TO THE PRUDENT CABBAGE EATERS OF NORTHERN ITALY. IT IS A VERY CLEVER WAY TO TURN A LEAN, DRY, RELATIVELY INEXPENSIVE CUT OF PORK INTO A MOREISH COMESTIBLE AND A GREAT WAY TO USE UP WHITE WINE LEFTOVERS. IT IS A DISH THAT TASTES LIKE THERE IS MORE TO IT THAN THERE IS — THE WAY THE WINE INFUSES THE CABBAGE, THE GARLIC INFUSES EVERYTHING AND THE PORK IS MOISTENED AND TENDERIZED BY THE WINE. PORK HAS AN AFFINITY WITH SWEET FRUIT (APPLE SAUCE, ET AL.), AND AN ACCOMPANYING GLASS OF RELATIVELY CHEAP, RIPE MERLOT ACTS AS A FRUITY CONDIMENT. **SERVES 4**

Ingredients

FOUR pork leg steaks
ONE TABLESPOON olive oil
FOUR CLOVES garlic, halved
125 ML (4 FL OZ/ $^1/_2$ CUP) white wine, preferably riesling
HALF a cabbage (savoy is best)

Method

Give the pork steaks a bash with a meat mallet to make them more or less the same thickness — aim for about 3 mm ($^1/_8$ in). Heat a large heavy-based frying pan with the olive oil over medium heat and brown the pork steaks and the garlic, being careful not to burn the garlic. This process should take about 5 minutes. Pour the wine over the meat and garlic and add the finely sliced cabbage and some generous grinds of black pepper. Cover with a lid and simmer for a further 30 minutes. If the liquid doesn't cover the meat or evaporates, top it up with a mixture of wine and water. Serve with a couple of boiled small waxy potatoes, skin on.

Pimento and pork

THIS IS PORK FOR THOSE WITH A PENCHANT FOR THE PIQUANT. WITH NONE OF THOSE SWEET, STICKY FLAVOURS THAT USUALLY BESMIRCH PORK CHOPS, SUCH AS APPLES, MAPLE SYRUP OR HONEY, THESE ARE CHOPS DESIGNED FOR RED WINE. THE PAPRIKA GIVES SOME INTERESTING SPICE AND EARTHINESS AND THAT MAKES IT GO NICELY WITH EARTHY RED BLENDS OF GRENACHE, SHIRAZ AND MOURVEDRE, OR GSM'S AS THEY'RE KNOWN IN THE BUSINESS. **SERVES 4**

Ingredients

ONE TABLESPOON paprika
TWO OR THREE CLOVES garlic, crushed
TWO TABLESPOONS olive oil
FOUR pork chops, about 2 cm (³⁄4 in) thick (loin chops are good but shoulder chops will do)
500 ML (17 FL OZ/2 CUPS) white wine

Method

Mix up the paprika, garlic and olive oil and rub well into both sides of the chops. Pour the wine over, cover with plastic wrap and let sit in the fridge for a day or two. When you're ready to cook, heat the grill of a barbecue until it's really hot, then put the chops on. Depending on the thickness of the chop, about 5 minutes per side should do it. Meanwhile, pour the marinade into a small frying pan and boil uncovered, until it is reduced to the consistency of gravy. Serve the chops with rice and pour the marinade over the top.

Migas

THIS IS THE FAMOUS RECYCLED BREAD DISH OF THE DRY ALENTEJO PROVINCE OF PORTUGAL — 'THE BARREN, ANGUISHED PLAINS OF REPENTANCE', AS ONE GUILTY POET CALLED IT. ALENTEJO IS THE WORLD CAPITAL OF FRUGAL COOKING AND MIGAS PRETTY MUCH SUMS UP THE WHOLE ETHOS. THIS USE OF STALE BREAD AND CHEAP CUTS OF PORK IS FRUGALITY AT ITS FINEST. IT GOES VERY WELL WITH YOUNG, INEXPENSIVE SHIRAZ. **SERVES 4**

Ingredients

750 G (1 LB 10 OZ) boneless pork spare ribs or
pork chops, chopped into chunks
THREE CLOVES garlic, finely chopped
TWO red chillies, finely chopped
A DRIZZLE of olive oil
ONE lemon, juiced
FOUR SLICES bacon
ONE LOAF stale, crusty bread

Method

Rub the pork pieces with the garlic, chilli and a little oil and squeeze over the lemon. Leave overnight, or as long as feasible. Cut the bacon into pieces and fry with the pork in batches in a frying pan, removing them as they cook and keeping the fat in the pan. Meanwhile, cut the bread into slices and place the slices in a bowl. Pour over enough boiling water to cover, and mash the bread with a wooden spoon. Add a sprinkle of salt and season with the fat from the pan. In Portugal, migas is cooked in an earthenware casserole dish but a modern frying pan works well, if a little less romantically. Over medium heat, pour the mushy bread into the pan and cook until it starts to form an omelette-like base. When that happens, give the pan a shake. The migas is ready when it's cooked on the outside but moist in the middle. Serve the migas with the meat on one large plate with the meat juices poured over the top, hand out forks and let everyone tuck in.

Plateless
pork and polenta

THIS IS A DISH THAT TAKES YOU BACK TO YOUR CHILDHOOD — IT'S MUD PIES FOR GROWN UPS. IT INVOLVES COOKING UP A PILE OF POLENTA AND A VAT OF SAUCE, POURING BOTH ONTO A TABLE AND TUCKING IN WITH A FORK. OBSESSIVE-COMPULSIVES AND HYGIENE FREAKS WILL HATE THE WHOLE IDEA, AS DO HEALTH AUTHORITIES WHEN IT'S DONE IN RESTAURANTS. IT'S LOADS OF FUN, A GREAT WAY TO SPREAD COMMUNICABLE DISEASES, RUIN A TABLE AND, IF YOU'RE FEEDING A LOT OF PEOPLE, SAVE ON WASHING UP. RED WINE IS OBLIGATORY AND CHEAP, GUTSY BLENDS ARE THE GO. NOTE: THIS RECIPE CAN BE EATEN OFF A PLATE BUT IT DOESN'T TASTE NEARLY AS GOOD. **SERVES 6**

Ingredients

2 KG (4 LB 8 OZ) pork forequarter chops
250 ML (9 FL OZ/1 CUP) olive oil
SIX CLOVES garlic, finely chopped
TWO GLASSES unwooded white wine
TWO TABLESPOONS tomato paste (concentrated purée)
1 KG (2 LB 4 OZ) mixture of red and green capsicums (peppers)

THREE small red chillies
A DASH of red wine vinegar
450 G (1 LB/3 CUPS) polenta
freshly grated provolone piccante or pecorino cheese
ONE table (old laminex covered tables are better than expensive wooden antique ones)

Method

Remove the fat from the pork and cut into fork-friendly pieces. Heat 4 tablespoons of the olive oil in a saucepan over medium heat and brown the pork. Add the garlic, reduce the heat to low and cook for about 10 minutes. Mix in the white wine and add the tomato paste to the pan. Put the lid on and simmer for 30 minutes. Now for the capsicums. Core and cut them into strips about 3 mm (1/8 in) wide. Seed and julienne the chillies and fry in another pan with the capsicums in the rest of the oil until soft. Add a dash of red wine vinegar, cook off and then add the capsicums and chillies to the meat. Simmer for another 30 minutes, or until the meat is tender. If things start to look a bit dry, loosen it up with a mixture of half water and white wine.

The polenta. Boil 3 litres (105 fl oz/12 cups) well-salted water in a large saucepan, add the polenta and stir for about 30 minutes, or until the polenta starts to be a coherent blob and pulls away from the side of the saucepan. If it gets a bit thick, add a bit more water.

Plonk the polenta on the table, make a big well in the middle, pour the sauce inside, top with a sprinkling of cheese and tuck in.

Cebollas rellenas

TRADITIONALLY, THE NOTION OF STUFFING VEGETABLES WITH MINCED THINGS WAS A WAY TO SAVE ON HOUSEHOLD EXPENDITURE AND WASHING UP. LEFTOVERS WERE JAMMED UP AND INTO WHATEVER FRUIT OR VEGETABLE HAPPENED TO BE AVAILABLE OR ABUNDANT. EVENTUALLY RECIPES LIKE CEBOLLAS RELLENAS DEVELOPED INTO HAUTE CUISINE. BUT THAT WAS 400 YEARS AGO AND THESE DAYS IT'S NOT MODISH TO SERVE A STUFFED ONION AT A SOPHISTICATED DINNER PARTY — WHICH IS A VERY GOOD REASON FOR ITS INCLUSION IN THIS BOOK … AND THE FACT THAT IT GOES FANTASTICALLY WITH SANGIOVESE. **SERVES 4**

Ingredients

EIGHT brown onions
FOUR TABLESPOONS milk
100 G (3½ OZ / 1 CUP) coarse dry breadcrumbs
160 G (5½ OZ) minced (ground) pork
ONE TABLESPOON chopped flat-leaf (Italian) parsley
TWO CLOVES garlic, chopped
ONE TEASPOON unwooded white wine
TWO eggs, beaten
olive oil

Method

Slice off the tops and bottoms of the onions and peel them down to the tender flesh. Heat some well-salted water in a saucepan and simmer the onions for about 15 minutes. Take the onions out and keep the water. Heat the milk and soak the breadcrumbs in it until soft. Mix in the pork, parsley, garlic, white wine, eggs (keeping a little for brushing the onions) and a good pinch of salt. Scoop the centres out of the onions and pack the meat mixture inside. Brush the onions with the reserved egg. Place the onions in a baking dish with the filling end upwards. Pour the hot onion water into the dish to half cover the onions and bake for about 30 minutes in a preheated 180°C (350°F/Gas 4) oven. Serve with greens and crusty bread.

Chapter 7
The Sheep

'Walking cutlets', Louis XVI

The sheep is a rare beast in that it can clothe as well as feed. You can say that of alpacas, mohair goats and probably Old English sheepdogs, but none of these creatures can boast four roasts, four racks, three types of chop — chump, loin and forequarter — cutlets, shanks and back strap — or milk that makes piquant cheese. It's no surprise that Australians aren't the only race to hitch a ride.

The sheep has much going for it. Observe the barren lambscapes of Australia's wide brown land and you'd think the sheep can live on dirt. And it's almost true — some of the most challenging country produces the best sheep meat. Saltbush lamb is the famous local example. The saltbush grows where nothing else will and helps to reduce dryland salinity, yet sheep can live on it. Saltbush-fed sheep produce meat that not only tastes better, but is leaner than pasture-grazed lamb. It's an environmentally benign symbiosis of plant and animal. The French equivalent to saltbush lamb is the *pre sale* lamb of Brittany. The sheep feed on the salty marshlands and end up at the *boucherie* pre-seasoned. Perhaps the most famous example of sheep adaptation is the fat-tailed sheep of the Middle East. The tail is like the hump on a camel — it stores fat, which acts as an emergency store in times of drought — and has become a delicacy in itself. It's a breed of sheep that goes back to the Old Testament era. When God asked Abraham to sacrifice his first-born child and a ram was substituted, doubtless it was one with a fat tail.

By contrast, Australia is merino-centric. Before the latest drought, the estimated ovine population was 100 million sheep (by contrast, New Zealand grazes 45 million sheep) of which 80 million were merinos. There are four different strains of merino — even a cool-climate one. Introduced to Australia back in 1796, 'the Spanish sheep', as it was called, was much better suited to Australia's hot, arid climate than the English breeds. The merino revolutionized sheep farming in Australia and now a basic division exists between the breed of the sheep destined for the closet or the table. While the merino supplies fleece, the rams of English descent, such as poll dorsets, are used with merino ewes to sire prime lambs.

There has been a multitude of thorny ovine issues over recent years — the wide-comb shearers strike of the 1980s, the spread of Ovine Johne's disease and the present debate over mulesing, to name a few. But the debate that never goes away is when is lamb lamb? By taste and even by appearance it's not very difficult to tell. Mutton can be identified by smell alone. The oldest evidence of domesticated sheep is a find of bones dating back to 9000 BC. The majority of the bones came from sheep that were under one year old. It seems that even way back then, young lamb tasted better than old lamb.

In very basic terms a lamb is not a lamb when it has teeth. The dictionary defines 'hogget' as a sheep that has not been shorn, and aged between 10 months and two years old, while 'lamb' is the meat of a young sheep with no permanent teeth. According to most Australian jurisdictions, a hogget is a ewe or a wether not showing secondary sex characteristics and that has cut one — but not more than two — permanent incisor teeth. Hence the slang for hogget, 'two toother'. However, these definitions are not universal. In New Zealand, a lamb is any sheep under 12 months of age — teeth or no teeth. This causes no small amount of friction on export markets where Kiwis brazenly trade hogget as lamb.

Domestically 'hogget' is a dirty word and 'lamb' is a generic that covers both. In a perfect world with perfect butcher shops hogget and lamb would be labelled as such and you'd be able to choose between them; milder tasting lamb for racks, cutlets and short-loin chops; and darker, strongly flavoured hogget for braises, curries and roast legs. Until that world exists, size is the best guide. If the leg is large and looks like it has clocked up a few kilometres in the paddock, it's hogget. If it's small, dainty and pink, it's lamb.

● ● ● ● ● ● ● ● ● ● ● ●

Yummy lamb curry

TWO OF CURRY'S MAIN MODUS OPERANDI ARE TO: 1. MAKE CHEAP (EVEN SLIGHTLY HIGH) CUTS OF MEAT EDIBLE AND 2. MAKE A SMALL AMOUNT OF MEAT FEED A LOT OF PEOPLE. THIS RECIPE FULFILS THE MISSION STATEMENT PERFECTLY. THE LAMB IS HIGHLY FLAVOURED WITH SPICES AND THEREBY DISGUISED, AND THE POTATO THICKENS THE CURRY AND PADS IT OUT. THIS CURRY CAN BE A BIT OF A WINE KILLER. RED WINE WORKS BEST, ESPECIALLY FRUITY, ROUNDER STYLES. SAVE YOUR BEST REDS FOR ANOTHER DISH AND DON'T GO FOR ANYTHING TOO TANNIC OR OAKY. **SERVES 4**

Ingredients

750–900 G (1 LB 10 OZ–2 LB) lamb forequarter or leg chops
THREE CLOVES garlic
1/2 A THUMB of ginger
ONE large onion
THREE dried chillies or three fresh ones

THREE TABLESPOONS Keens curry powder
1/2 TEASPOON ground fennel
125 ML (4 FL OZ/1/2 CUP) olive oil
EIGHT cardamom pods, bruised
TWO star anise
500 G (1 LB 2 OZ) potatoes, diced

Method

Remove the fat and chop the lamb into fork-friendly pieces. Chop the garlic, ginger, onion and chillies very finely or whiz in a food processor. Mix the curry and the ground fennel with enough water in a cup to make a paste. Heat a tablespoon of the olive oil in a heavy-based flameproof casserole dish, add the cardamom and star anise and fry for about a minute over medium heat, or until fragrant. Add the garlic, ginger, onion and chilli mixture. Stir-fry until the onion starts to become transparent, then add the curry paste. Mix it all together and fry for a minute or so. Throw in the diced lamb and brown it, making sure to coat all the pieces in the mixture. Pour in enough water to just cover the meat and add 2 good pinches of salt. Set it at a slow simmer until the meat is just tender, about 1 hour. Add the potatoes and simmer until the potatoes are soft and the sauce is thickened. Adjust for seasoning and serve with basmati rice.

Frank
shanks

THE LAMB SHANK, ONCE ONE OF THOSE BITS OF BUTCHERY FETCHED FROM THE BEAST IN THE BACK ROOM, NOW FEATURES FRONT AND CENTRE IN PRETTY POLYSTYRENE PACKS. IN PRICE PER KILO TERMS, IT'S UP THERE WITH THE WHOLE LEG OF LAMB. EVEN AT THIS PRICE IT OFFERS TREMENDOUS VALUE. SERVED UP ON A BED OF BEANS IT IS A TRULY SATISFYING FEED AND ONE SHANK PER PERSON IS PLENTY. THE GLUEYNESS AND STICKINESS OF THE BEANS AND SHANK MEAT WITH A TOMATO-BASED SAUCE FINDS A WONDERFUL MATCH WITH GUTSY REDS, ESPECIALLY CABERNET SAUVIGNONS. **SERVES 4**

Ingredients

TWO TABLESPOONS olive oil
TWO onions, finely chopped
FOUR CLOVES garlic, finely chopped
ONE TABLESPOON Spanish smoked paprika
FOUR lamb shanks
TWO TINS (800 G/1 LB 12 OZ) tomatoes
FOUR bay leaves
1 LITRE (35 FL OZ/4 CUPS) Greg's quick chicken stock (page 73)
FOUR carrots, chopped

Method

Heat the oil in a flameproof casserole dish over medium heat and cook the onions and garlic until soft. Add the paprika and the lamb shanks, browning them and coating them with the paprika and onion mixture. Add the tomatoes, bay leaves and enough chicken stock to cover the shanks by about 2 cm (³/₄ in), and bring to a slow simmer for about 3 hours. Add the carrots and simmer for another 20 minutes. Serve on a bed of beans — either 'Baked beans the old way' (page 54) or a dry version of 'Fagioli al fiasco' (page 51) — and plenty of crusty bread to mop up the juices.

Peasy lamb

THIS IS A TASTY ITALIAN TAKE ON THE LAMB STEW — A COMBINATION OF LAMB, PEAS AND A SAUCE THICKENED BY EGG. THE YOUNGER THE LAMB THE BETTER THIS DISH WORKS, AND IT'S A GOOD MATCH FOR CAB MERLOT BLENDS. **SERVES 4**

Ingredients

1 KG (2 LB 4 OZ) lamb chump chops
THREE TABLESPOONS olive oil
ONE large onion, finely chopped
1/2 GLASS white wine
310 G (11 OZ/2 CUPS) frozen peas
FOUR eggs
50 G (1¾ OZ/½ CUP) grated parmesan cheese
ONE LARGE HANDFUL flat-leaf (Italian) parsley, chopped

Method

Cut the lamb into fork-friendly pieces, removing as much fat as is feasible. Heat the olive oil in a frying pan over medium heat and brown the lamb and the onion for about 10 minutes. Pour in the wine and cook for another 15 minutes, then add the frozen peas and cook until tender — about another 10 minutes. Season with salt and pepper and remove from the heat. In a bowl, lightly beat the eggs, then add the parmesan cheese and parsley to the eggs and mix together. Gently and slowly add the egg mixture to the meat, stirring at the same time. The heat of the meat should cook the eggs and turn it into a thick sauce. Serve with 'Garlic mash' (page 135).

Venetian
lamb's fry

ONE BAD LIVER DISH CAN TURN YOU OFF FOR LIFE. TOO THICKLY CUT, NOT QUITE DONE, A BIT OLD AND THAT'S IT — NO LIVER FOREVER AFTER. ONCE UPON A TIME JUST ABOUT EVERY HOUSEHOLD IN THE COUNTRY COOKED LAMB'S FRY. NOW, MOST COOKS UNDER 60 DON'T EAT IT AND CERTAINLY DON'T KNOW HOW TO COOK IT. THE SECRET LIES IN THIN SLICES, LOTS OF CRISPY BITS AND A LITTLE DISGUISE. THE CLASSIC AUSSIE VERSION USES BACON, BUT HERE, HEAPS OF ONION HELPS DIMINISH THE LIVERISHNESS. ADD SOME GARLIC MASH AND A GLASS OF LIGHT- TO MEDIUM-BODIED RED WINE AND YOU'LL BE LOOKING AT THE OFFAL DEPARTMENT OF YOUR LOCAL BUTCHER WITH A KEENER EYE. **SERVES 4**

Ingredients

ONE lamb's liver
60 G (2¼ OZ / ½ CUP) plain (all-purpose) flour
125 ML (4 FL OZ / ½ CUP) olive oil
FOUR large onions, thinly sliced
THREE TABLESPOONS white wine vinegar

Method

Trim the skin, the veiny and yucky bits off the liver and cut into slices no more than 4 mm (⅛ in) thick. Get a plastic bag and put the flour in there with some generous grinds of black pepper and a couple of big pinches of salt. Add the liver slices to the flour bag and give it a good shake so that the liver is well dusted. Heat half the olive oil in a frying pan and soften the onions so that they go limp and clear but don't brown or burn. Remove the onions and keep them warm. With the frying pan heat on high, add the remaining oil and fry the liver for about a minute on each side. Remove and keep warm. Pour the white wine vinegar into the pan and scrape up all the bits into a sort of gravy — if it's not thick enough add a tiny bit of flour from the plastic bag you dusted the liver in. Serve the slices of liver on top of piles of onions and pour a little of the gravy over the top, and serve with 'Garlic mash' (page 135).

Lamb in
a pan

THIS IS A PORTUGUESE METHOD OF COOKING LAMB OR KID. IT'S AN UNUSUAL COOKING TECHNIQUE, AND IS NOT SO MUCH FRIED AS STEAMED IN OIL. THE LAMB ABSORBS THE GARLICKY OIL, BECOMING EXCEEDINGLY JUICY. YOUNG, FEISTY CABERNETS GO ESPECIALLY WELL WITH IT. **SERVES 4**

Ingredients

ONE small leg of lamb
ONE TEASPOON black peppercorns
FOUR CLOVES garlic
125 ML (4 FL OZ / 1/2 CUP) olive oil

Method

Bone out the leg of lamb (or ask your butcher to do it) and cut into small fork-friendly pieces. Using a mortar, pound the peppercorns and then the garlic with 1 teaspoon of coarse salt. Rub this paste into the lamb pieces and leave overnight, or as long as possible.

Place the pieces in a large heavy-based saucepan with the oil, cover with a lid and cook over low heat for about 45 minutes. Hold the lid on and give it a shake from time to time. When you suspect that all the liquid has been absorbed, have a look. If the lamb is browned and all the liquid is gone, it's ready to eat. Serve with plain rice.

Chapter 8
The Cow

I used to work on my Uncle Bill's dairy farm and between 1972 and 1980 I saw some huge changes. Milking herds increased from 25 to 50 to 100 cows and farmers who once had a Peggy, a Betsy and a Polly soon ran out of names. Uncle Bill, and many like him, adopted the royal system. Peggy III would be milked alongside her daughters Peggy IV, V and VI. But with herds ever increasing it wasn't long before things got beyond the average farmer's facility in roman numeracy and that's when dairy cows began to be identified by numbers.

At about the same time the biggest revolution since the invention of the milking machine occurred — the herringbone milking shed. With the herringbone system, the farmer stood in a pit at eye level with the cows' teats — thus alleviating the dairy worker's greatest grief, back pain. With this system you could milk 80 cows twice a day and not know which cow you were milking. After a while you'd recognize number 5674's udder by sight but you wouldn't know her once she was out in the paddock. It was a system less painful on the back and much less painful on the heart. When 5674's milking days were over and the cattle truck arrived to take her to the abattoir, unless you looked at her udder you didn't feel a thing.

This all has a point. What was happening on Uncle Bill's farm is symbolic of what has been happening in butcher shops and supermarkets over the last 20 years. Meat has become de-animalized. Gone are the beasts hanging on hooks in full view awaiting that special request, which the butcher would facilitate with his knife in front of you. Meat has been prettified on polystyrene. It sits on absorbent napkins under special lighting pretending for all the world that it doesn't come from a dead cow.*

Once upon a time, a skilled housewife knew the different cuts of meat and, if you gave her an apron and a sharp knife, she'd probably do a fair job of carving up a carcass. These days few people below the age of 50 know their way around a butcher shop, let alone a side of beef. But for the cook this is crucial knowledge. Matching the meat to the method is 90 per cent of the job. Some cuts of meat should only be minced or ground, some are underrated and many are criminally overpriced. So in the interests of this vital information staying in circulation, following is an explanation of the different cuts of meat and what they're good for.

a side of beef

the hindquarter

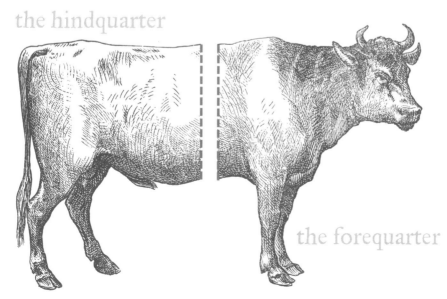

the forequarter

After an animal has been 'processed' at the abattoir, it is sawn into two sides that can then be divided into four quarters.

the hindquarter

GRAVY BEEF is taken from the boned out leg of the cow. It's the best choice for braises, slow-cooked beef curries and that sort of thing. It's no good for fast cooking, it takes time, but for both flavour and texture, it's worth it.

OSSO BUCCO is traditionally made from veal leg sawn straight across the bone. In Australia 'osso bucco' refers to any bit of meat cut this way. Both the veal and the beef version can be very useful in slow braises. The marrow from the bone adds flavour and texture to sauces.

ROUND STEAK comes from the flank and can be cut into steaks or made as a roast. It's lean and pretty-looking meat but dry and boring and best left on the shelf.

TOPSIDE comes from the inside of the hindquarter. Again, this is sold as a roast or as steaks but is best corned as silverside or minced (ground).

THE RUMP predictably comes from the upper part of the hindquarter. A tasty cut of beef, it's good for barbecuing and excellent for stir-fries. It has good flavour and not too much fat.

THE FILLET is situated underneath the rump. It's one of the most highly rated cuts of beef but I'm not a big fan. It's expensive and tasteless; however, it is tender, and a good choice if you don't have your own teeth.

THE FLANK OR SKIRT STEAK lies on the inside of the hindquarter and is okay for braising.

THE LOIN is at the top end of the hindquarter and home to some great barbecue meat. From the loin comes the T-bone, porterhouse and sirloin — all A-rated cuts of steak.

the forequarter

SCOTCH FILLET lies within the ribs. It is a tastier substitute for the fillet steak.

RIB ROASTS also come from this bit of the beast. The standing rib roast, which contains the bone, is the best cut of beef for roasting.

RIB CUTLET OR ENTRECOTE is a favourite cut of steak in Italian and French butcheries. The bone adds flavour.

BRISKET lies around the ribs. It is a tasty, often fatty bit of meat that is best boiled or corned.

BLADE STEAK comes from the shoulder and includes cuts such as the blade roast (which is best ignored), the cross-cut blade (not bad for budget barbecue steak), and oyster blade steak (good for stir-fries).

CHUCK STEAK is under the blade. Along with gravy beef, it is the best all-purpose stewing steak.

* An interesting footnote to this story. I went to France in 1989 and worked on a dairy farm. It felt like I was back at home. The same black-and-white Friesian cows, the same Alpha Laval milking equipment, but the difference was that it was like stepping back 20 years. No herringbone milking sheds and no numbers. You bent down to milk and the cows were called Marguerite, Françoise and Isabel; and French butcher shops were old-fashioned blood-and-guts affairs with every bit of the beast on view and for sale.

Polpettone

THIS IS AN ITALIAN MEAT LOAF. IF THOSE WORDS MAKE YOU THINK OF BAD 80'S MUSIC OR MINCE IN THE SHAPE OF A LOAF, THINK AGAIN. THE ITALIANS KNOW HOW TO DO THIS STUFF AND AFTER CONSUMING THIS DISH THE WORDS 'MEAT LOAF' WILL NEVER MEAN THE SAME AGAIN. YOUNG FRUITY REDS LOVE IT. **SERVES 4**

Ingredients

500 G (1 LB 2 OZ) minced (ground) pork
500 G (1 LB 2 OZ) minced (ground) veal
FOUR eggs
ONE onion, diced
TWO CLOVES garlic, finely chopped
ONE SMALL HANDFUL flat-leaf
(Italian) parsley, chopped
TWO hard-boiled eggs
75 G (2 1/2 OZ) bacon or ham
75 G (2 1/2 OZ) provolone cheese

Method

Mix the minced meats with the raw eggs, onion, garlic and parsley, and season generously with salt and pepper. Lay half of this mixture in a terrine tin or loaf-shaped cake tin. Roughly chop the bacon or ham, boiled eggs and provolone and lay this mixture on top. Cover with the other half of the meat mixture. Put the terrine in a baking tray and fill with enough boiling water so that it comes halfway up the sides of the terrine. Bake in a preheated 180°C (350°F/Gas 4) oven for about 1 1/2 hours. Serve hot, and the leftovers cold.

Pot au feu

A KITCHEN CIRCA 1150. AT THE FIREPLACE, BITS OF MEAT HANG IN A CAULDRON FROM PIECES OF STRING. ALSO IN THE POT IS A BUNCH OF VEGIES SIMMERING AWAY. WHAT'S BEING COOKED IS POT AU FEU, A PRIMORDIAL, TASTY WAY TO FEED A LOT OF PEOPLE. IT'S PROBABLY ONE OF THE OLDEST EXISTING RECIPES AND THERE ARE AS MANY WAYS TO MAKE POT AU FEU AS THERE ARE VILLAGES IN FRANCE. IT'S EVEN SPREAD BEYOND THE BORDERS TO NORTHERN ITALY. THE PIEDMONTESE VERSION IS CALLED BOLLITO AND CAN HAVE ANYTHING FROM A CALF'S HEAD TO A PIG'S TROTTER IN THE POT. FOR THIS RECIPE FIVE HOURS, A VERY LARGE POT AND A LOT OF PEOPLE ARE PREREQUISITES. IT'S A DISH THAT WILL FLATTER MOST MEDIUM-BODIED RED WINES, BUT STEER CLEAR OF ANYTHING TOO OAKY OR TANNIC. **SERVES 12**

● ● ● ● ● ● ● ● ● ● ● ●

Ingredients

2 KG (4 LB 8 OZ) beef brisket, without too much fat

FOUR bay leaves

TWO OR THREE thyme sprigs

ONE BUNCH flat-leaf (Italian) parsley, tied together

TWO celery stalks with leaves

TWO TEASPOONS mixed black and white peppercorns

FOUR onions, peeled

SIX CLOVES garlic, crushed

SIXTEEN carrots

ONE ham hock

ONE fresh chicken

FOUR chorizo sausages

TWELVE small potatoes

TWELVE parsnips

SIX leeks

Method

For tradition's sake and so you can pull out the bits of meat easily, tie a piece of string around the brisket and secure to the handle of a huge heavy-based saucepan. Add the herbs, celery, peppercorns, 2 teaspoons of salt, whole onions, garlic and 4 chopped carrots, and cover with cold water. Slowly bring to the boil, skimming off the scum as it comes to the surface. Turn down to the barest simmer. After an hour, tie a piece of string around the ham hock and truss the chicken with string, tie them to the handle and add them to the pan. Leave it to tick over for another 2 hours, add the chorizos, tied with string, and cook for another 30 minutes. Everything should be tender and tasty at this stage.

Chop the remaining vegies into large pieces and parboil them in another saucepan for 10 minutes. Then, in a high-sided saucepan half-filled with the cooking stock, simmer them for another 15–20 minutes, or until they're tender.

Remove the meat from the stock and place on a large plate or board for carving at the table, medieval style. Serve up the vegies the same way and drizzle them with some stock. Serve with mustard or 'Sauce de sorges' (page 34).

Beef bouillon
with ginger

A CONTAINER OF THIS BOUILLON SHOULD BE IN EVERYONE'S FRIDGE OR FREEZER, FOR COLDS, FLU, SOUPS AND STEWS, OR JUST WITH NOODLES. IT'S THE GINGER THAT MAKES THE MAGIC AND PROVIDES THE HEALING. IF SYMPTOMS PERSIST, SEE YOUR DOCTOR. **MAKES ABOUT 3 LITRES (105 FL OZ/12 CUPS)**

Ingredients

500 G (1 LB 2 OZ) oven-browned beef bones
ONE THUMB of ginger, thinly sliced
ONE large onion, quartered

Method

Throw all the ingredients into a large saucepan, add 3 litres (105 fl oz/12 cups) cold water, a couple of big pinches of salt and bring to the boil. Skim off any scum and simmer for about 1 hour, or until the onion has dissolved and the ginger slices are tender.

Rustic
terrine

IT'S A TOSS-UP WHETHER THIS SHOULD BE IN THE PIG, THE COW OR THE CHICKEN CHAPTER — IT USES BITS AND PIECES OF EACH. THIS IS PICNIC FOOD. A LITTLE BIT SPREAD ON A LARGE PIECE OF CRUSTY BREAD WITH SOME ACCOMPANYING POTATO SALAD IS THE WAY TO EAT IT. CONSUMED THIS WAY IT'S ONE OF THE FEW THINGS THAT GOES WITH SPARKLING RED WINE. **SERVES 4**

Ingredients

250 G (9 OZ) lean beef
250 G (9 OZ) pork belly
250 G (9 OZ) chicken livers
125 G (4½ OZ) butter
ONE large onion, diced
THREE CLOVES garlic, finely chopped
100 ML (3½ FL OZ) Armagnac or brandy

ONE egg, beaten
TWO TABLESPOONS lemon juice
ONE TEASPOON chopped thyme
ONE TEASPOON chopped oregano
ONE TEASPOON chopped rosemary
250 G (9 OZ) bacon
TWELVE bay leaves

Method

Put all the meat except the bacon in a food processor and mince (grind) together well, then place in a bowl. Melt the butter in a frying pan over low heat and cook the onion and garlic until soft but not coloured. Add to the meat. Pour the Armagnac into the pan and cook over medium heat until a third has evaporated, then pour the rest into the meat and mix together with the beaten egg, lemon juice, all the herbs except the bay leaves, a large pinch of salt and some generous grinds of pepper. Line a 30 x 12 cm (12 x 4½ in) terrine with slices of bacon — with enough overlapping the terrine to cover the top as well. Pour in the meat mixture and fold the bacon over to seal the top. Decorate with bay leaves, cover with foil and place in a baking tray. Pour boiling water into the tray so that it comes halfway up the sides of the terrine. Cook in a preheated 180°C (350°F/Gas 4) oven for 2 hours. Uncover for the last 10–15 minutes. Remove from the oven and cool. Cover again with foil and put a brick or something similar on top to compact it. Refrigerate for at least 12 hours.

Veal agnolotti
with sage oil

IF YOU'VE GOT A BIT OF TIME ON YOUR HANDS, OR HAVE A FANTASTIC BOTTLE OF
CHIANTI, OR WANT TO SEDUCE SOMEONE WITH YOUR COOKING SKILLS, THIS IS
THE DISH. THE GENTLE FLAVOURS OF VEAL AND SAGE AND THE SUMPTUOUS
TEXTURE OF THE AGNOLOTTI MAKE A WORTHY STAGE ON WHICH YOU AND
YOUR CHIANTI CAN STRUT. **SERVES 4**

Ingredients

ONE TABLESPOON good olive oil
ONE large onion, very finely chopped
250 G (9 OZ) minced (ground) veal
FOUR bay leaves
ONE TEASPOON lemon zest
ONE TABLESPOON grated parmesan
cheese, plus extra to top
ONE egg, beaten

FOR THE PASTA
250 G (9 OZ/2 CUPS) plain
(all-purpose) flour
TWO eggs
FOR THE SAGE OIL
TWO TABLESPOONS good olive oil,
or butter if preferred
ONE BUNCH sage leaves

Method

Heat the olive oil in a saucepan over medium heat and cook the onion until softened. Add the veal and cook until browned, breaking up the lumps as much as possible. Add the bay leaves and 250 ml (9 fl oz/1 cup) water, cover with a lid, reduce the heat to low and simmer slowly, stirring regularly. After 30 minutes remove the lid and cook off the extra liquid. Remove from the heat, throw out the bay leaves and cool. When it's cool to touch, fold in the lemon zest, parmesan and beaten egg.

For the pasta, sift the flour into a bowl, make a well in the centre and break the eggs into the well. Mix in with a wooden spoon, then use your hands. Knead the dough, trying to spread the eggs through the flour. If after all your efforts it's still a bit dry, add a smidgeon of water — but not too much, you don't want it too wet. When you've kneaded it into a rough dough, form it into a ball and cover with plastic wrap. Leave it for an hour for the starch and egg to do the work.

After an hour give it another knead on a floured board. If you've got a pasta machine use that to run the dough into thin strips. Otherwise, do your best with a rolling pin. Using a glass or cup with a 6–8 cm (2½–3¼ in) diameter opening, cut the dough into circles. Put about a teaspoon of the veal mixture on half the rounds and then cover with another round. Press down the edges with a fork to make a pretty pattern. (You're aiming to make 16–20 agnolotti.) Heat a large saucepan of well-salted water to a rolling boil. Cooking time will depend upon the thickness of your pasta but err on the side of too long rather than too little. Use one of the agnolotti as a tester.

Now for the sage oil. Heat the olive oil in a saucepan and add a few dozen sage leaves. Fry them gently until they're crisp. Plate up the agnolotti, pour over the sage oil, garnish with the crispy sage leaves and a few gratings of parmesan.

Post-modern
steak sandwich

HERE'S AN OPEN STEAK SANDWICH WITH THE LOT … IT'S A FEAST AND GOES VERY WELL WITH RED WINE THAT HAS A FEW YEARS UNDER ITS BELT. **SERVES 4**

Ingredients

FOUR CLOVES garlic, finely chopped
200 G (7 OZ) butter
ONE LARGE HANDFUL flat-leaf (Italian) parsley, finely chopped
ONE SMALL LOAF crusty white bread, cut into 2–3 cm (3/4–1 1/4 in) slices
THREE onions, sliced into rings
ONE TABLESPOON olive oil

TWO TABLESPOONS balsamic vinegar
400 G (14 OZ) champignons (baby button mushrooms), sliced
FOUR spring onions (scallions)
125 ML (4 FL OZ/1/2 CUP) red wine
1/2 TEASPOON cornflour (cornstarch)
FOUR small, thick steaks (sirloins or porterhouses are good here)

Method

Preheat the oven to 180°C (350°F/Gas 4) and the barbecue grill to high. Blend the garlic, butter (reserving 1 teaspoon for the mushrooms) and parsley together in a bowl. Spread the garlic butter liberally on both sides of each bread slice. If you've got some left, smear a bit on the outside for extra crusting. Pack the slices tightly together and cover with foil. Put it in the oven (or in a barbecue with a lid, if you prefer) for 15–20 minutes, or until the butter has melted through and a decent crust has formed.

Meanwhile, in a frying pan sauté the onions slowly in the olive oil until they caramelize. Add the balsamic and cook it off. Keep the onion rings warm. Cook the mushrooms, reserved butter and chopped spring onions in another pan over low heat until they soften. Add the wine, cover with a lid and simmer for 20–30 minutes. When done, take the lid off and cook a little more to reduce the sauce. If needed, add the cornflour mixed with a little water to thicken the sauce.

Meanwhile, cook the steaks. On the barbecue, cook one side until beads of blood form on the top, then turn and cook the other side for a few minutes. Let it rest for a moment and assemble the sandwich: a slice of garlic bread, balsamic onions, then the steak topped with the mushroom sauce.

Chapter 9
The Vegetable

The potato, the cabbage and the cauliflower — three pale table amigos; each an answer to the cruel cry of hunger, each a vehicle for flavour and each with a story to tell.

the potato

At school I did a unit called 'Agriculture'. One of the requirements for passing the course was to plant a crop in the school vegie patch and bring it to fruition. I chose to plant potatoes. I dug my patch, buried 5 kilos (11 lb) of seed potatoes and forgot about them until it was time to dig them up. What a harvest! Bag after bag of beautiful pink spuds emerged from the fecund earth. I fed the class, the street, the suburb … we were eating pontiacs for weeks.

I had accidentally discovered the reason why the potato, a newcomer in vegie history, has become so widespread — it has a huge potential to feed.

Discovered growing in the Andes about 1530, the spud has been cultivated by the Peruvians since about 3000 BC. It was useful at the higher altitudes where corn wouldn't grow. Soon after the conquistadors arrived in South America the potato was being cultivated in Spain. It was grown near Seville in 1539 and from there they spread to Galicia — a much better climate — and then onto Italy. Apparently, it was Sir Walter Raleigh who first introduced potatoes to Ireland when he planted them on his Irish estate in 1586.

They spread, but not because they were liked. The French in particular weren't fond. Diderot, the author of an 18th century encyclopaedia wrote:

This root, no matter how you prepare it, is tasteless and floury. It cannot pass for an agreeable food, but supplies a food sufficiently abundant and sufficiently healthy for men who ask only to sustain themselves. The potato is criticized with reason for being windy but what matters windiness for the vigorous organisms of peasants and labourers.

But even for peasants it was suspect. For a long time the spud was thought to cause leprosy. They were eaten green, and in those days solanine — the compound in potatoes that is poisonous — was much higher. It didn't poison anyone, but it did give them a rash — hence leprosy.

The Irish potato famine did nothing for the reputation. The potato had been a blessing for the poor Irish who were constantly starving. Just a small plot of spuds could feed a family year round. But even before the potato famine, Irish cooking was being criticized by the English for being too spud-centric. When the potato blight hit Europe in 1845 the Irish suffered more than most.

It has been the chip — the frying of potato in oil — that has bought the potato wide acceptance and fame. How the chip came to be is the source of much conjecture. Not surprisingly, its origins are linked to fried fish.

There is a recipe for fried potatoes in a French cookbook dated 1770. However, the Spanish claim that the Galicians were frying spuds to eat with their fishy diet long before this and they passed it on to the Belgians; and the Belgians claim that they invented *frites* all by themselves. The Belgians certainly have the best story.

It goes like this:

The poor and homeless inhabitants of Liege used to eat small fried fish that they'd net in the Meuse river. But in cold snaps, when the river froze over, they couldn't fish anymore, so they'd cut potatoes the same size as the little fish and fry them. A local entrepreneur, whose name [no joke] happened to be Frits, started selling these fried potatoes in a roadside stall and so the frite *and takeaway food were invented almost side-by-side.*

the cabbage

Diogenes, the Greek philosopher, once said to a friend: 'If you lived on cabbage, you would not be obliged to flatter the powerful'. I've tried it. A variety of factors — penury and curiosity being the main two — obliged me to exist almost solely on cabbage in various forms for a period of about six months. At the time I wasn't familiar with the particular advantage of this diet that Diogenes points out.

According to Greek mythology, the cabbage came about like this: Dionysius, the God of Wine came upon Lycurgus, the founder of Spartan Law and anti-alcohol zealot, digging up his grapevines. In his fury, Dionysius tied Lycurgus to a vine and blinded him. Lycurgus cried and from his tears grew cabbages. So began the link between alcohol and cabbage. For centuries cabbage was thought to be an antidote to drunkenness. Even now, in vodka-drinking countries, cabbage is sometimes consumed during skulling sessions.

The cabbage has always been considered the vegetable of the poor. The nobility and the royalty of the medieval period prided themselves — at the cost to their digestions — on abundant meat eating and rarely admitted to eating the vegetable. Cabbage's big moment at the royal table came in the 14th century when Charles VI of France was served cabbage as a first course by his very brave chef. According to legend this was no ordinary cabbage. It was the famous 'senlis' cabbage, which apparently did not smell like cabbage at all but had an odour somewhere between musk and ambergris. Unfortunately, the senlis cabbage has since become extinct so we can't verify that.

The cabbage has now spread all over the world and is available in many cultivars. The purple cabbage, so a 17th century French story goes, came to be when an unmarried but obviously pregnant girl from Perigueux was walking home balancing a cabbage on her large belly. The streets are narrow and on this day they were lined with virtuous-minded people who heckled the fallen girl mercilessly. The bishop happened to see this and, taking pity on the girl, took the cabbage from her, wrapped it in his cloak and escorted her home. When he unwrapped it and handed it back, the cabbage had taken on the colour of the Episcopal robes.

the cauliflower

Many things were lost, broken or destroyed during the Dark Ages when the Visigoths, Vandals and Barbarian hordes pulled the Roman Empire to bits — literature, art, buildings, an entire culture and even the cauliflower.

The cauliflower is basically a highly evolved cabbage. Horticultural selection accentuates the growth of the flowers rather than the leaves, and it seems that lack of cultivation more than anything else caused it to disappear during the Dark Ages. It took another millennium before it reappeared in Europe. Cauliflower is mentioned at the end of the 16th century in a list of new vegetables published in Germany, and first enters the French language as *chou fleur* in the early 17th century. In the 18th century it was a very fashionable vegetable and a favourite at Louis XIV's court. Louis XV even had a cauliflower dish named after his mistress, Madame du Barry. But those glory days are long gone and we have entered a new, barbarous Dark Age where the cauliflower is once more a neglected vegetable, scorned by trendy chefs, and boiled to death by negligent cooks. Please give it a chance — cauliflower can be very tasty.

Indian split
peas and
cabbage

HERE'S AN IMAGINATIVE CABBAGE DISH THAT USES TWO INGREDIENTS THAT DON'T USUALLY GO TOGETHER OUTSIDE OF A SOUP. THE HUMBLE SPLIT PEA AND SOME INDIAN FLAVOURINGS GO TOGETHER TO CREATE A NUTTY, TEXTURED VEGIE DISH THAT CAN BE SERVED ON ITS OWN WITH RICE OR AS AN ACCOMPANIMENT TO SOME MEATIER FARE. **SERVES 4**

Ingredients

THREE TABLESPOONS olive oil

ONE TEASPOON black mustard seeds

TWO TEASPOONS cumin seeds

FOUR curry leaves, fresh if you've got them, otherwise dried is okay

TWO dried chillies

110 G (3¾ OZ/½ CUP) green split peas, soaked overnight

HALF a sugarloaf cabbage, cored and sliced chunkily

½ TEASPOON ground turmeric

ONE HANDFUL coriander (cilantro) leaves, chopped

Method

Heat the oil in a frying pan over low heat. Add the mustard and cumin seeds and heat until the mustard seeds pop. Add the curry leaves, dried chillies and drained split peas and fry over medium–low heat for about 5 minutes. Add the cabbage and turmeric, and keep frying slowly until the cabbage is cooked. Season with salt, add the coriander and serve.

Cavolo in agrodolce

HERE'S A QUICK AND EASY ITALIAN WAY TO MAKE SOMETHING A BIT SPECIAL FROM THE HUMBLE CABBAGE. THIS DISH CAN LIFT A SIMPLE BARBECUED CHOP OUT OF THE EVERYDAY. ADJUST THE SUGAR IF YOU THINK IT NEEDS IT. **SERVES 4**

Ingredients

ONE onion, diced
ONE CLOVE garlic, finely chopped
ONE TABLESPOON olive oil
ONE TIN (400 G/14 OZ) tomatoes
ONE savoy cabbage, finely chopped
ONE TABLESPOON red wine vinegar
TWO TEASPOONS sugar

Method

In a large heavy-based saucepan sauté the onion and garlic in olive oil over medium heat. When the onion is golden, add the tinned tomatoes and break them up with a wooden spoon. Cook for 5 minutes, then add the cabbage. Add a pinch of salt and 5 grinds of pepper and the vinegar, then cover with a lid and simmer for 10–15 minutes. Add the sugar and simmer for another 5 minutes before serving.

Tortilla de patatas

I ONCE LIVED ALMOST ENTIRELY ON TORTILLA DE PATATAS FOR A PERIOD OF TWO WEEKS — ANOTHER EXPERIMENT. I WAS ON A MISSION TO FIND THE BEST TORTILLA DE PATATAS IN SPAIN. EVENTUALLY I NARROWED IT DOWN TO A DAGGY CAFÉ IN JEREZ DE LA FRONTERA, WHERE THEY SHOWED RERUNS OF OLD BULLFIGHTS ON A CRACKLY TV OVER THE BAR. THIS RECIPE IS AS CLOSE AS I COULD GET TO THE OLD CAFÉ'S VERSION AND I SUSPECT CIGARETTE SMOKE, AND A BIT OF KITCHEN 'TERROIR' ARE THE MISSING INGREDIENTS. NOWADAYS I EAT TORTILLA DE PATATAS AT HOME WATCHING THE FOOTY OR WHEN I WANT TO BE REMINDED OF SPAIN. WHEN CONSUMED COLD, A DRY FINO SHERRY IS EXCELLENT, WHEN EATEN WARM, CHOOSE LIGHT-BODIED RED WINE. **SERVES 4**

Ingredients

750 G (1 LB 10 OZ) waxy potatoes
375 ML (13 FL OZ/1½ CUPS) olive oil, for deep frying,
plus extra for cooking the tortilla
SIX eggs

Method

Slice the potatoes finely and dry them with a cloth. Heat the oil in a deep saucepan with a lid and add the potatoes. Deep-fry over medium heat for about 30 minutes with the lid on, stirring occasionally. The potatoes should be soft but not golden — you're not making chips. Remove the potatoes and drain. Sprinkle with coarse salt. Beat the eggs together and add more salt. Mix the potato slices with the eggs. Heat enough oil to cover the bottom of a frying pan on medium–low heat and add the potato and egg mixture. Give the pan a shake to stop the mixture sticking and cook for about 3 minutes, or until just set. Now (this is the tricky bit), with a plate on top, invert the frying pan so the tortilla is on the plate, cooked side up. Slide it back into the frying pan and cook the other side for another 2–3 minutes. The ideal tortilla is slightly runny in the middle and not rubbery. As with bullfighting, practice makes perfect.

Spicy cauli

THE CAULIFLOWER IS A FANTASTIC FLAVOUR VEHICLE. HERE SOME INDIAN SPICES AND A BIT OF POTATO TRANSFORM THE RATHER BORING VEGETABLE INTO A SUMPTUOUSLY FLAVOURED FOOD. SERVE IT VEGETARIAN STYLE WITH RICE OR AS AN ACCOMPANIMENT TO A CURRY. **SERVES 4**

Ingredients

ONE cauliflower
THREE TABLESPOONS olive oil
$1/2$ TEASPOON black mustard seeds
$1/2$ TEASPOON cumin seeds
FOUR potatoes, diced
TWO CLOVES garlic, finely chopped
ONE green chilli, seeded and chopped
$1/2$ TEASPOON ground cumin
$1/2$ TEASPOON ground coriander
$1/4$ TEASPOON ground turmeric

Method

First break the cauliflower into its individual florets and discard any bits that are too stalky. Heat the oil in a heavy-based saucepan over medium–low heat and add the mustard and cumin seeds and cook until the mustard seeds pop. Add the potatoes and stir-fry for a couple of minutes before adding the garlic and chilli, the remaining spices and the cauliflower florets. Stir-fry for a minute or so, then cover with 80–100 ml ($2^{1}/_{2}$–$3^{1}/_{2}$ fl oz) water. Bring the mixture to the boil, cover with a lid and simmer for about 8 minutes, or until the cauliflower is tender but still firm and all the water has evaporated. Give a liberal seasoning with salt and serve.

Buttered
savoy

CABBAGE IS CABBAGE YOU MIGHT THINK. NOT SO. COOKED IN A HOME-MADE STOCK AND LUBRICATED WITH SOME SPICY DAIRY FAT, A CABBAGE CAN TASTE LIKE SOMETHING COMPLETELY DIFFERENT. ESPECIALLY WHEN IT'S A SAVOY — THE KING OF THE CABBAGES. **SERVES 4**

Ingredients

ONE savoy cabbage

375 ML (13 FL OZ / 1½ CUPS) Greg's quick chicken stock (page 73)

50 G (1¾ OZ) butter

ONE TEASPOON dry-roasted cumin seeds

ONE TEASPOON Spanish smoked paprika

Method

Cut the savoy in half and, using a V-cut, remove the stem from both halves. Halve these halves again. In a large saucepan bring the chicken stock to the boil, then add the cabbage. The cabbage should be sitting in 1–2 cm (½–¾ in) of stock. Cover with a lid and cook on high heat for 4–5 minutes, or until the cabbage is just tender. Drain and keep warm. Meanwhile, melt the butter with the cumin and paprika in a saucepan. Heat gently for a few minutes. Dish out the cabbage and drizzle the spicy butter over the top.

Garlic mash

GARLIC IS COSMOPOLITAN. A MERE WHIFF OF THE MIRACULOUS HERB CAN MAKE A DISH TRAVEL BETWEEN CONTINENTS. POKE A SLIVER OR TWO INTO A ROAST LEG OF LAMB AND THAT LAMB WILL MOVE (FLAVOURWISE) FROM GREAT BRITAIN TO BRITTANY. HERE, THE GARLIC IN THE MASH ADDS AN ITALIAN ACCENT TO MASHED SPUDS. THERE'S AN ADDED FLAVOUR AND SOPHISTICATION TO THE MASH THAT SEEMS INCOMPLETE WITHOUT A GLASS OF RED. **SERVES 4**

Ingredients

1 KG (2 LB 4 OZ) sebago potatoes
THREE CLOVES garlic
250 ML (9 FL OZ/1 CUP) milk
A KNOB of butter (optional)

Method

Peel the spuds and cut into small chunks to make them cook faster. Put them in a saucepan with the garlic, cover with water and bring to the boil. Simmer until the potatoes start to fall to bits. Drain in a colander and return to the pan. Add the milk and butter (if cholesterol isn't an issue), then mash both spuds and garlic into a purée. Adjust for salt and serve.

Barbecued
spuds with green olives

THIS IS A NIFTY WAY TO GET A MEDITERRANEAN ACCENT INTO THE SPUDS. SERVE THIS WITH SOME CUTLETS MARINATED IN GARLIC AND OLIVE OIL. **SERVES 4**

Ingredients

1 KG (2 LB 4 OZ) waxy potatoes
FOUR TABLESPOONS green olives (the cheap stuffed ones are okay)
ONE TABLESPOON olive oil, plus extra for oiling the barbecue

Method

Cut the spuds into rough cubes, then parboil them for about 5 minutes. Chop the olives in half and mix them with the spuds and olive oil. Heat an oiled barbecue plate and cook the spuds and olives until the potatoes are golden brown and crispy.

Cauliflower
murcia

LIFT THE LID OFF THIS DISH AND YOU'LL HAVE PEOPLE TUCKING INTO CAULIFLOWER LIKE THEY NEVER HAVE BEFORE. LIKE MOST CAULI CREATIONS IT'S NOT PARTICULARLY PRETTY BUT THE BEAUTY IS FOR THE OLFACTORIES NOT THE OPTICS. WITH OLD-FASHIONED SPANISH COOKING TECHNIQUES SUCH AS A FRIED BREAD THICKENED SAUCE AND THE TRUSTY, HONEST FLAVOURS OF GARLIC AND PAPRIKA, THE BORING OLD BRASSICA TURNS INTO SOMETHING QUITE EXOTIC. THE SPANISH EAT THIS WITH MEAT AND EGGS AND USE THE LEFTOVERS IN TORTILLAS. **SERVES 4**

Ingredients

ONE cauliflower
TWO TEASPOONS lemon juice
THREE TABLESPOONS olive oil
TWO THICK SLICES crusty bread
TWO TEASPOONS paprika
TWO CLOVES garlic
ONE TABLESPOON chopped flat-leaf (Italian) parsley

Method

Break the cauliflower into florets and put them into a bowl with the lemon juice. Heat the oil in a heavy-based flameproof casserole dish and fry the bread until golden, then remove. Add the paprika to the oil and 375 ml (13 fl oz/ 1½ cups) water. When boiling, add the cauliflower with a large pinch of coarse salt. Simmer with the lid on until the cauliflower is tender. Meanwhile, crush the garlic, parsley and fried slices of bread using a mortar and add to the cauliflower. Stir and adjust the seasoning. Cook for a few minutes until the sauce blends and thickens, then serve.

Chapter 10
The Lemon

When I think about the lemon I think about its many uses. And when I think about the many uses for lemons I think about Tony Joe White. Tony is the bloke who wrote 'Polk Salad Annie', a song Elvis made famous and that I suspect Tony has lived off ever since. Tony is the godfather of swamp music.

I had seen him perform many times and was reasonably familiar with his stage props. There was the chair he sat in (Tony never played standing up), there was the papier-mâché 'gator that moved its jaws when Tone sang 'Polk Salad Annie' and 'Gumbo John'; there was the well-used 60's stratocaster complete with the strap made from a rattlesnake — head and all — and there was the old tweed fender valve amp. On top of the amp, within reach of Tony's chair there was usually a glass of water, two or three harmonicas in different keys and a capo; but on this night there was something else. Four quarters of what looked like a lemon of the eureka variety sat in a neat line. Tony ambled on stage, strapped on his guitar, grabbed one of the lemon quarters and jammed it in his mouth. He sucked on it like he was squeezing a high note out of his harmonica. 'I've got a touch of swamp fever,' he drawled as he placed the dejuiced skin and pith on his amp and got down to business. Tony went through seven lemons and most of his repertoire that night, and as far as I could tell, sang perfectly.

Stricken with a nasty bout of swamp fever (a bad cold), I've tried Tony's lemon method — and it works. Somehow the lemon juice frees the constriction of the vocal chords. But being able to sing with a face contorted from sucking a lemon is another skill altogether …

The lemon is a truly amazing fruit. It can heal, clean and preserve. You could call it nature's natural acid. But you'd be wrong. The lemon is an invention. An ancient hybrid of the citron and an Indian lime. Lemon historians theorize that it first came into cultivation in the West, from the foothills of the Punjab in Pakistan and India.

While the Romans used and cultivated the lemon, the Visigoths, Vandals and other marauding tribes did not. They had no use for a fruit you couldn't eat straight off the tree. So, with the fall of the Roman Empire in the 4th century, the lemon also fell into decline.

When Pope Urban II preached the First Crusade in 1095 to a bunch of landless French knights there were no lemons in France. The knights galloped to Jerusalem to kill Saracens and free the Holy Sepulchre, and the booty included lemons. Lemons and unbelievers have a long connection. It was the Moorish invasions of Spain and Sicily during the 8th and 9th centuries that bought the lemon tree back into Europe.

There are three main types of lemon: the lisbon, meyer and eureka. The lisbon is, of course, originally from Portugal. It was introduced to Australia in 1824 and selections from it later exported to California, where they regard it as the Australian lemon. It's the tough, rough-skinned, pale yellow lemon in gardens all over Australia. It's an excellent lemon for zesting.

The meyer lemon is a cross of a lemon, orange and mandarin. It was found growing near Beijing in 1908. The fruit is more spherical than the average lemon and turns a pale orange colour when mature on the tree. It's a pretty lemon, but for cooks the meyer is a dud. The juice lacks zing and the skin is no good for zest.

The eureka lemon is the preferred lemon of coastal areas. It's nearly thornless, cropping all year round in hot coastal areas, with the bumper season in early to mid Autumn. The fruit has a rough skin that is often ribbed and has highly acidic flesh, which yields loads of juice. The fruit also has a prominent nipple at its base — an excellent lemon for juice, zest and singing when you have a cold.

Lemon and
pecan teacake

THIS IS A TANGY TEACAKE THAT CAN NOT ONLY BE UTILIZED AT AN ALCOHOL-FREE AFTERNOON TEA, BUT ALSO AS A DESSERT WITH ICE CREAM, TOPPED WITH STRIPS OF GLAZED LEMON ZEST AND A STICKY WHITE WINE. **SERVES 4**

Ingredients

185 G (6½ OZ/1½ CUPS) plain (all-purpose) flour
220 G (7¾ OZ/1 CUP) sugar
ONE TEASPOON baking powder
125 G (4½ OZ) butter
TWO eggs
125 ML (4 FL OZ/½ CUP) milk
ONE lemon, zested and juiced

60 G (2¼ OZ/½ CUP) chopped pecans
55 G (2 OZ/¼ CUP) caster (superfine) sugar

GLAZED LEMON ZEST
ONE lemon
ONE TABLESPOON sugar

Method

Sift the flour into a bowl and mix in the sugar, baking powder and a pinch of salt. Cut the butter into cubes and rub into the flour mixture with your fingers. In another bowl, beat the eggs with the milk, then fold into the flour. Finally, mix in the zest of the lemon and the pecans. Grease and line a 21 x 15 cm (8¼ x 6 in) baking tin with baking paper, pour in the batter and place in a preheated 180°C (350°F/Gas 4) oven. Cook for 1 hour, or until a skewer inserted into the cake comes out clean. Mix the caster sugar with the juice of the zested lemon and pour over the cake while still warm. Leave it to cool in the tin. For the glazed lemon zest, remove the zest from the lemon with a small knife and cut the pieces into matchstick-sized strips. Add to a saucepan with 125 ml (4 fl oz/½ cup) water and the caster sugar and simmer over medium heat for about 5 minutes, or until the zest strips become clear. Remove the cake from the tin, then spread the glazed zest over the top.

Preserved
lemons

THE PRESERVED LEMON IS A STRANGE THING. BEFORE YOU'VE USED THEM YOU WONDER WHAT YOU WOULD DO WITH SUCH A THING. ONCE YOU HAVE USED THEM YOU WONDER HOW YOU EVER DID WITHOUT THEM. IN AUTUMN, WHEN EVERYONE WITH A TREE IN THEIR BACKYARD IS GIVING THEM AWAY, IT'S THE THING TO DO. THE MAGIC INGREDIENT IS THE SALT, WHICH DRAWS THE JUICE OUT OF THE LEMON AND SOFTENS THE ZEST. THEY'RE READY TO USE IN ABOUT SIX WEEKS. RINSE OFF THE SALT AND DISCARD THE FLESH. USE THE ZEST TO LIVEN UP A SALAD OR CHICKEN DISH. **MAKES AS MANY AS YOU'D LIKE**

Ingredients

lemons, enough to fill your chosen jar
lemon juice

Method

Wash the lemons and cut them lengthways into quarters — but don't cut them all the way through. Remove the pips as best you can with a thin knife, and sprinkle plenty of coarse salt on the flesh inside the lemon. Close the fruit and pack the lemons, as tightly as you can, into a sterilized jar. Add freshly squeezed lemon juice to cover, screw the lid on tight and wait.

Santiago lemon
and almond cake

THIS COFFEE-FRIENDLY CAKE COMES FROM SANTIAGO DE COMPOSTELLA, THE FAMOUS PILGRIMAGE DESTINATION IN GALICIA IN NORTH-WEST SPAIN WHERE THE BONES OF SAINT JAMES RESIDE. THE TRAFFIC OF PILGRIMS FROM FRANCE TO SANTIAGO IN THE MIDDLE AGES IS THEORIZED TO HAVE RESULTED IN TEMPRANILLO — SPAIN'S MOST FAMOUS RED GRAPE VARIETY. TEMPRANILLO IS THOUGHT TO BE A MUTATION OF PINOT NOIR, WHICH CAME ACROSS THE NORTH OF SPAIN AS CUTTINGS CARRIED BY BURGUNDIAN PILGRIMS. HOWEVER, THERE IS NO THEORY AS TO HOW THIS VERY ARABIC-STYLED CAKE FOUND ITS WAY TO THE CATHOLIC NORTH-WESTERN TIP OF SPAIN. **SERVES 4**

Ingredients

FOUR eggs
100 G (3½ OZ) butter
165 G (5¾ OZ/¾ CUP) sugar
90 G (3¼ OZ/¾ CUP) plain (all-purpose) flour
ONE TABLESPOON baking powder
200 G (7 OZ/2 CUPS) ground almonds
ONE lemon, zested
icing (confectioners') sugar, to dust

Method

Beat the eggs with the butter and sugar. Stir in the flour and baking powder and gradually add 170 ml (5½ fl oz/⅔ cup) water. Finally, fold in the ground almonds and the lemon zest. Put into a greased 25 cm (10 in) round cake tin and place in a preheated 170°C (325°F/Gas 3) oven. Bake for 35 minutes, or until a skewer inserted into the cake comes out clean. Remove from the oven, allow to cool and remove from the cake tin. For true authenticity, cut a cross out of paper as a stencil, place on top of the cake and dust with icing sugar. Remove the paper cross and serve piously.

Saucy lemon pudding

SOMEONE ONCE DESCRIBED THIS DESSERT AS BREAST-FEEDING FOR ADULTS. A FAIRLY REVOLTING THOUGHT BUT YOU GET THE IDEA — IT'S COMFORT FOOD. BUT THERE'S SOMETHING ELSE. FEW DESSERTS GO AS HAPPILY WITH A REALLY GLUEY BOTRYTIZED DESSERT WINE. THIS PUDDING COSTS VIRTUALLY NOTHING TO MAKE, SO LASH OUT ON A REALLY GOOD STICKY. **SERVES 4**

Ingredients

100 G (3^1/$_2$ OZ) butter

180 G (6^1/$_2$ OZ) caster (superfine) sugar

TWO good lemons (tough and rough lisbons are best)

FOUR eggs

60 G (2^1/$_4$ OZ/^{1}/$_2$ CUP) plain (all-purpose) flour

250 ML (9 FL OZ/1 CUP) milk

Method

Cream the butter and sugar until light and fluffy. If you don't have a food mixer you can use a hand-beater, but make sure your butter is very soft or it will take ages. Grate the zest from one of the lemons, then squeeze the juice from both. Separate the eggs and add the yolks to the creamed butter and sugar, then fold in the flour, milk, zest and lemon juice. Mix it up and add a little extra milk if it is too dry. Beat the egg whites to stiff peaks, then fold them in carefully. Scrape into a greased ovenproof bowl. Stand the bowl in a baking dish half-filled with hot water and put into a preheated 180°C (350°F/Gas 4) oven for about 1 hour, or until the top is golden and has a sponge cake texture. Serve out of the bowl with cream or ice cream and the aforesaid sticky.

Chapter 11
The Apple

Although we always think of Eve biting into something that looked like a pink lady, if you check your copy of the Bible you won't find any mention of apples — well not in Genesis 3 anyway. What Adam and Eve ate was the 'fruit from the tree of knowledge of good and evil' and the fruit of that particular plant is not described. But from the Beatles record label to the Apple Mac, the apple has always been as much a symbol as a fruit so it's no surprise that it was adopted as the fruit consumed in the Garden of Eden that ruined things for the rest of us. Imagine if Eve had eaten a forbidden banana — things might have turned out very differently. An apple in a lunchbox symbolizes health, a bowl of apples on a table symbolizes well-being, and a rotten apple in a barrel, the spread of evil. It is a fruit pregnant with meaning.

Speaking of which, the apple has a long tradition as a fertility symbol. When Solon was in charge of Athens he decreed that there would be no feasting for the bridal couple excepting an apple that they had to share before going to bed. Solon knew that love prefers an empty stomach. The Greeks had other marital roles for apples. Throwing your beloved an apple was a proposal of marriage. If she caught it she accepted. In medieval Germany an apple could be made into a love charm but the recipe was a bit tricky. It was believed that if you ate an apple that had been marinated in the perspiration of the woman you desired, she'd fall in love with you. How you gathered so much sweat in a cool climate, from a woman with whom you were obviously not intimate isn't explained. Possibly it was not a love potion but a cure. The process of gathering cupfuls of your sweetheart's sweat and steeping an apple in it might very well cool your own desire.

Despite this rather bizarre use, the apple is the most utilitarian fruit. It can be eaten Eve-style straight off the tree, fermented, stewed, puréed, dried, baked and, with its ability to be cool stored, eaten year-round.

Since first being cultivated by the Egyptians in 1300 BC, varieties of the apple have increased exponentially. Pliny the Elder in the 1st century AD could number 36 different varieties. Now there are tens of thousands. However, you won't find near that many varieties at your local supermarket. Apples are subject to fashion and most of the apples we eat are relatively recent horticultural inventions. Here's a guide to the main players in the market at present.

BONZA Born in Batlow, New South Wales, in 1950, the round, red bonza was the epitome of the lunchbox apple in the 70's and 80's, but is now falling from favour. Its flesh is very white and crisp and it stores slightly better than a Jonathan. It's ripe, just before the delicious apple, in early to mid autumn.

BRAEBURN The braeburn came to being in Hastings, New Zealand, in 1981. It's a tangy, juicy apple and remarkable for the fact that it doesn't brown quickly after being cut. Consequently it's a good apple for salads. It's ripe just after the bonza and stores relatively well, although with age can develop bitter pips.

DELICIOUS If you feel like you've been eating delicious apples long before any of these other varieties, you have. The delicious dates back to Iowa in the US in 1880 and is the world's most popular apple. Its popularity is due in part to its long storage capability. It's ripe in early autumn.

FUJI The unique tasting fuji came into being in Japan in 1939 but the war interfered and it wasn't named and introduced to the rest of the world until 1962. A cross between ralls and delicious, you can taste the latter parentage in the fuji's juicy sweetness. Fujis are ripe in early to mid autumn.

GALA (ROYAL GALA) Ripening in late summer, you'll find new season's galas in the supermarkets alongside last season's delicious. Born in Wairarapa in the North Island of New Zealand in 1934, the gala is a cross between kidd's orange red and golden delicious. A good eating apple when fresh; they don't store well.

GOLDEN DELICIOUS The golden delicious came about by accident in West Virginia in 1890. It's one of those apples that divide consumers down the middle. I'm a fan. It does bruise easily but small, crisp new season's versions are hard to beat. It ripens about the same time as delicious and doesn't store particularly well.

GRANNY SMITH The granny is Australia's gift to the apple world. It popped up in Granny Smith's backyard in Eastwood, New South Wales, back in 1868. Granny Smith nurtured the sapling and the rest is history. It is, without question, the best cooking apple, with good acidity and fine texture when stewed. It's ripe in mid to late Autumn.

JONATHAN A common misconception is that the jonathan came from Johnny Appleseed's apple planting crusade in the US in the 1800's. The jonathan has actually been traced back to a seedling found on a farm at Woodstock, about a century before the legendary rock concert. A late summer ripener, new season's jonathans are much better eating than their stored counterparts.

JONOGOLD As the name suggests, the jonogold is a cross between a golden delicious and a jonathan. It was created in the United States in 1948 but wasn't actually released into the apple world until 1968. With a sweetness unbalanced by any tang and a rough texture, the jonogold doesn't come highly recommended. It's ripe a couple of weeks after delicious.

LADY WILLIAM The lady william is another accidental apple occurring in Donnybrook, Western Australia, in 1935. One of the latest ripeners in the seasonal calendar, and as such not suitable for cold climates, the lady william can be fickle and finding a good one a bit of a hit or miss. When they're good they're good and when they're not they're good for the horse.

PINK LADY 'Pink lady' is actually a registered brand name, the real name of this increasingly popular apple is 'cripps pink', having been created by one John Cripps at the Stoneville Research Station in Western Australia in 1973 by crossing golden delicious with lady william. The pink lady is sweet, crisp and uniquely flavoured — it's hard to beat as an eating apple when fresh. It's a late ripener coming off the tree in late autumn. It stores for about four months.

SUNDOWNER Developed at the same time as the pink lady and by the same crossing and the same bloke, 'cripps red', as it is really called, is a completely different fruit to the pink lady. Not as sweet and with coarser flesh, it ripens a little bit later and stores for a bit longer. The pink lady is far superior.

● ● ● ● ● ● ● ● ● ● ●

Apple and
walnut cake

THIS IS A VERY EASY CAKE TO MAKE. IT'S A 'THROW IT ALL TOGETHER AND WHACK IT IN THE OVEN' NUMBER. A WINNER WITH COFFEE OR TEA, IT'S ALSO NOT BAD WITH ICE CREAM AS A DESSERT. IN THAT CASE, A SMALL GLASS OF LIQUEUR TOKAY IS A GOOD IDEA. **SERVES 4**

Ingredients

THREE small, tangy granny smith apples
250 G (9 OZ) sugar
TWO eggs
100 G (3½ OZ/1 CUP) walnuts
85 G (3 OZ/²/₃ CUP) self-raising flour
85 G (3 OZ/²/₃ CUP) plain (all-purpose) flour
ONE TEASPOON bicarbonate of soda (baking soda)
ONE TEASPOON ground cinnamon
125 G (4½ OZ) butter

Method

Crank the oven up to 200°C (400°F/Gas 6). Peel and cut each apple in half, then core and slice them. Put the apple slices in a bowl with the sugar and give it a good stir. Add the eggs and mix well. Stir in the whole nuts, the flours, bicarb and cinnamon. Melt the butter and stir into the mixture to make a sort of lumpy batter. Pour into a well-greased 1.5 litre (52 fl oz/6 cup) ring mould or Kugelhopf * tin. Bake in the oven for 10 minutes, then turn down to 180°C (350°F/Gas 4) and cook for another 50 minutes. Leave to rest for 10 minutes before turning it out onto a wire rack to cool.

* A Kugelhopf is a fluted ring tin that gets its name from the famous yeast cake of Alsace — the gugelhopf.

Granny
pudding

YOU CAN WHIP UP THIS DESSERT IN AN INSTANT AND, IF YOU'RE REASONABLY COORDINATED, TALK AND LAUGH WITH YOUR GUESTS AS YOU PREPARE IT. IT'S ANOTHER DISH THAT GOES WELL WITH A RIVERINA STICKY. **SERVES 4**

Ingredients

60 G (2¼ OZ/½ CUP) plain (all-purpose) flour
TWO TEASPOONS baking powder
115 G (4 OZ/½ CUP) caster (superfine) sugar, plus extra to dust
55 G (2 OZ/½ CUP) ground almonds
TWO eggs
250 G (9 OZ/1 CUP) sour cream
THREE granny smith apples
slivered almonds, for sprinkling on top

Method

In a bowl, sift the flour, baking powder and caster sugar, then mix in the ground almonds. In a separate bowl, whisk the eggs and blend in the sour cream. Add the flour mixture to the egg mixture and beat until smooth. Peel and cut each apple in half, then core and slice them. Grease a baking dish and pour in half the batter. Scatter half the apple slices on top. Add the rest of the batter, then the rest of the apples on top. Dust with caster sugar and sprinkle with slivered almonds. Bake in a preheated 180°C (350°F/Gas 4) oven for 45 minutes. Cool for 10 minutes and serve with cream, custard or ice cream.

Baked frigged apples

THE BAKED APPLE COMES IN MANY FORMS. THIS RECIPE USES THE CLASSIC BAKING APPLE — GRANNY SMITH — AND DRIED FIGS INSTEAD OF SULTANAS (GOLDEN RAISINS). IT WORKS BEST WITH TART, NEW SEASON GRANNYS. **SERVES 4**

Ingredients

FOUR large granny smith apples
25 G (1 OZ) butter
55 G (2 OZ/1/4 CUP FIRMLY PACKED) soft brown sugar
1/2 TEASPOON ground cinnamon
175 G (6 OZ/1 CUP) chopped dried figs
115 G (4 OZ/1/2 CUP) caster (superfine) sugar
TWO TABLESPOONS bush honey (leatherwood if you can get it)
ONE lemon, zested and juiced

Method

First core the apples. Mix together the butter, brown sugar, cinnamon and figs. Stuff each apple with the mixture so that it's tight and spilling out the top. Meanwhile, combine 125 ml (4 fl oz/1/2 cup) water, the sugar, honey and lemon zest and juice in a saucepan and heat until the sugar dissolves. Put the apples in a baking dish, pour the lemon and sugar liquid over the top and bake in a preheated 180°C (350°F/Gas 4) oven for 30 minutes, or until the apples are soft but not collapsing. Serve with a little cream or ice cream.

Tarte tatin

THIS CLASSIC FRENCH DESSERT IS CREDITED TO TWO SPINSTERS WHO RAN A RESTAURANT IN FRANCE'S LOIRE VALLEY. LIKE MOST GREAT INVENTIONS IT CAME ABOUT BY ACCIDENT. THE ELDER SISTER, STÉPHANIE TATIN (1838–1917), WAS BUSY ONE DAY AND PUT THE APPLES IN THE PIE DISH BEFORE THE PASTRY. SHE PUT THE PASTRY ON TOP AND STUCK IT IN THE OVEN AND VOILA! THE UPSIDE-DOWN APPLE TART WAS BORN. STEPHANIE TATIN WOULD NOT HAVE ENJOYED THE LUXURY OF A FOOD PROCESSOR SO THIS RECIPE IS A BIT DIFFERENT TO HERS BUT THE SPIRIT IS THERE. IT GOES VERY WELL WITH BOTRYTIZED RIESLING. **SERVES 4**

Ingredients

FOR THE PASTRY
170 G (6 OZ) plain (all-purpose) flour
100 G (3½ OZ) chilled butter, chopped

100 G (3½ OZ) sugar
EIGHT golden delicious apples
100 G (3½ OZ) butter, chopped

Method

Combine the flour, chilled butter and a pinch of salt in a food processor. Add 3 tablespoons cold water and whiz until the mixture comes together. Give it a quick knead on a floured board and shape it into a ball. Cover with plastic wrap and refrigerate for 1 hour. Meanwhile, mix the sugar with 2 tablespoons hot water in an ovenproof 24 cm (9½ in) frying pan and cook over low heat, without stirring, until the sugar is dissolved and begins to turn to golden caramel. Remove from the heat, stir in the butter and set aside for 10 minutes.

Peel and cut each apple in half, then core and slice them. Arrange them prettily in the pan. Return the pan to medium heat and cook, pressing the apples into the caramel with a spatula. Cook for 20 minutes, or until a deep golden caramel forms, which is bubbling over the apples. Remove from the heat.

Roll out the pastry on a lightly floured surface to a size slightly larger than the pan and place the pastry disk on top of the apples, then turn down the edges. Cook in a preheated 220°C (425°F/Gas 7) oven for 30 minutes, or until the pastry is golden and cooked through. Leave for 10 minutes before turning out on a serving plate. Serve with ice cream or thick cream.

index

Greg Duncan Powell lives perched on a hill overlooking the sea on the New South Wales south coast. He tastes wine for a living, cooks for fun and occasionally writes books. A father of two small children, he is also a surfer, windsurfer, musician and sometimes tree surgeon, and complains that his life is stressful and very busy.